All rights reserved. No part or this book may be reproduced or transmitted in any form or by any means, electronic or mechanical, including photocopying, recoding or by any informational storage and retrieval system, without permission in writing from the publisher.

Published By:

M. PUBLICATIONS LLC

www.mpublications.com

Manufactured in the United States of America

ISBN: 978-0-9829326-9-8

Edited by:

Andre Ricardo -
www.AndreRicardo.com

Copyright ©2016 Gwen Collins-Womack

ACKNOWLEDGMENTS

I would like to acknowledge all of the people who contributed to the Kickstarter campaign: Beverly Collins Adams, Patrina Ross, Alcides Flores, Sean & Ila Moodie Miguel and Imara Hernandez, Alvester, Miriam Hernandez and many others, even when you didn't know me.

I would like to acknowledge all of the people, past and present, who played a part in my destiny: good, bad and ugly. You were chosen, and I thank you. You made me think, you made me grow and I am always grateful to have experienced the "Experience," that is now a part of my yesterday.

Lastly, I would like to acknowledge all of the people who read the first copy and will read the second, third and fourth, YOU ROCK!

"Live while you are dying!"

Gwen Womack, July 2016

DEDICATION

I would like to dedicate this writing to all of the people I love and who loves me. It is you who gave me the strength to complete this work.

My husband, West Womack, who unselfishly motivated me and encouraged me to continue.

Magistrate Carol Fouty, a lifetime friend who knew me when.
Mrs. Carolyn Dorcas, my tutor, my guide through college and a rock-solid friend.
Katie Layne for being such a trooper and a stand-up friend.

To my children, Pedra and Warren, this is for you—for loving me still. And, always to my mother, Lila Mae and my grandmother, Cecil… I did it.

Andre Lawrence, my editor, it would not have been possible without you.
("BSAGW"!)
To Juliette Ross, my publisher, ("M Publications") thank you for the hand-off. I also thank you for believing I had a story to tell.

I want to especially thank my dear friends whom tirelessly supported my Kickstarter Video Campaign with their Academy Award winning acting: Wanda, Lisa, Brenda, Larry, Stephanie, Destiny, Addie and Mike. Thank you so very much.

To those who will follow my lead. Let's do this!

I dedicate this book to myself, for having the opportunity to experience The Experience. What a privilege!

EDITOR'S PREFACE

TWO: Pain and Peril picks up where ONE finished: bleeding profusely with cuts and bruises all over her body, Gwen Womack dug a hole in a swampy ditch to hide from two men who stood just above her, plotting what to do with her body after they had their way with it.

It's now the end of the 60's and Womack now resides in Charleston, West Virginia, a student of the then-newly formed Job Corps and the girlfriend of a local pimp and heroine user.

President Johnson's "War On Drugs," an undercover FBI informant, and a trail of blood leading to a dark passageway, are just a few of the most daring moments that happen in a span of just four years.

Believe me when I tell you, these are just a few.

The thrilling but outrageous life of Gwen Collins Womack continues.

1

As they approached The Lang Apartments, a young teenage girl ran ahead of them, quickly into the doorway. When Gwen and the woman came to the entrance, they saw ripples of red drops that lead through the doors and up the stairs.

Gwen and the homeless woman tiptoed carefully around the bloody stream. As they approached the second floor, they saw the young girl banging on Miss Delores' door. The bloodied footprints lead to Miss Delores', but Gwen couldn't tell where exactly the blood was coming from. Looking at the girl more intently, Gwen saw that the young woman's dress and legs were soaked in blood. They were coated in it as it continued to flow heavily and drain down to her feet.

Gwen turned to the strange woman, "Wait here; I'll be right back." Gwen rested her bag down next to the stairs and walked around the footprints to Miss Delores' door. She peeked inside but didn't see Dolly. When she lifted her head, she saw a room straight ahead down the hall with the open door. As she took a closer look, she saw a bed facing the door and the young woman face up on the bed.

Her feet were lifted up, pressed against the wall. Gwen thought the young girl believed the bleeding would stop if it stayed in her. Just then, a lady who came from another room walked into the hallway and saw the doorway only to see the young girl's feet making an imprint of blood on the wall, but when she saw the blood all over the bed spread, she screamed.

Gwen leaned back quickly, as not to be seen.

two

It was hard for Gwen to sleep in the taxi on her way home. She kept thinking about the moments after she escaped the ravine she fell in, and the fear of Robert Lee and Wally Smith making good on their threat to kill her and her family. Her adrenaline was still high but was relieved when she was able to catch a quick ride out from Mrs. Robinson's house. She didn't want to stay at her home any longer than she needed to be.

****

Gwen stayed at the Robinsons' house for about an hour. She had just enough time to drink a glass of water. Although the offer for the slice of a vanilla bundt cake, glazed with a butter-rum sauce was tempting, Gwen felt she'd be imposing if she accepted a slice. Instead, Gwen walked over to the stove to get a closer peek of it when Mrs. Robinson left the kitchen to make a call.

'Just a look and nothing more', Gwen told herself as she heard Mrs. Robinson arranging for a taxi. Before she walked away, Gwen saw a reflection of her midsection. She saw a small pouch where a flat stomach was not more than a couple of weeks ago. I must go on a diet, she said to herself, glancing at her reflection as she turned side to side.

****

Gwen had nodded off and was jolted awake by the bumps in the road that the mayor promised to fix several years before. The taxi driver rambled on and on about something, unaware that Gwen dozed off in the back. The only thing she remembered as they drove off was her thoughts on how bloated she felt. 'Why do I feel so gassy when I didn't have anything to eat since last night? That was more than twelve hours ago?'

She gripped her sides noticing both the love-handles, but also the scratches on her hands and arms. 'Why did they come after me? What did I do to give them the impression that I was some kind of ho? What will Jink do if I tell him? Will he go looking for them or would he blame me for going out?' It didn't all make sense to her. She looked up to see a familiar store. She was less than two minutes away from her apartment building, and the sleep that she missed had returned with a vengeance.

The taxi pulled up right in front of The Lang Apartments, and Gwen slowly got out of the car. As she stood up to reach into her back pocket, she noticed an older man, most likely in his seventies, who was blatantly staring at her. Gwen self-consciously looked down at herself and the high heels she held in her hands as she ran through the fields. They weren't any worse for the wear, but she paid too much money for them to get them damaged running over rocks, branches and whatever else was out there. She was not going to tear these shoes up, no sir.

Gwen continued to look at herself, she saw a few cut marks and different sections of peeled skin. She noticed the blue polyester pants she was wearing, which won her so many compliments when she walked into the clubs, now looked as if it were worn by the dingiest and grimiest mechanic, changing a flat tire in the middle of a mud storm.

She only had but a few crumpled up bills from her back pocket, but if it weren't for Mrs. Robinson pleading her case with the taxi service, those bills wouldn't have taken her very far. No sooner had she turned from the driver to hand him a few balled up pieces of paper when the old man approached her and stood barely two feet in front of her. He stood there silent for a moment looking her up and down, shaking his head as he observed her clothes, face and hair that was covered in dry mud.

"Young lady, I've been seeing you around here for quite some time now. I would see you over at that school," he said, as he pointed in a direction down the street, "Now, look at you. What happened to you, young lady?"

Gwen, startled by the confrontation,

"I... I... fell down this... this..."
"Girl, don't give me no excuses. We see your type every year. You got problems at home, your parents send you off, and you come here and you get yourself into trouble."
"I didn't mean to get into trouble... wait, can I explain what happened," Gwen said as she tried to pat down her hair and brush off as many stains as possible.
"You don't got to explain a darn thing to me. I seen you with that boy Jink or whatever he calls himself. What are you doing with a hoodlum like that? Don't you know he's trouble? Can't you see what you're getting yourself into?"
"Into what? Jink is my boyfriend." Gwen said with a puzzled

look on her face.

"Boy-O-boy! Look what you got yourself into now. Boyfriend, huh!"

The old man took half a step back and pierced her eyes with a pensive stare,

"Don't tell me that you didn't know that boy Jinkins is married? He's married to that girl..." The old man stared at the ground for a second,
"What's that girl's name... she's got a funny name... Wi-lutha... Wa-lenka.... Wu-thunka... oh, lord, what is her name.... Wilhemena! That's that girl's name, Wilhemena!"

"I heard of a Wilhemena, but I never met her," Gwen said as she studied his face trying to see if he was mistaken or just attempting to scare her away from Jink. "Are you sure, because my Jink is not married. He lives with his mother."

"How can I be so sure! How can I be so sure?"

He shook his head in disbelief then pointed his finger at her,

"Girl, how could you be so dumb? How could you be so dumb? I've known that boy and his family for as long as I as I've known myself. I know every member of that boy's family, and I can tell you right here that I've been knowing them before your momma would wipe that stuff out of your diaper. I'll tell you that much!"

For the first time, she began to think about her situation with Jink. She got the sense that this elderly gentlemen's words resonated some truth. 'Is Jink married? Why would he disappear for hours on end? Why would he not call or come by on some weekends? Where exactly does he work? When he told me that he needed to check his traps, what did that mean?' These thoughts quickly came to her mind.

"Don't you have anything to say for yourself, girl? You're just gonna stand there looking like a dummy? Say something!"

"Well, what do you want me to say? I don't have any proof that he's married. I don't know you, I've never even seen you before and you say all these bad things about Jink and me. How am I supposed to react to all of this?"

"Young lady... let me ask you a question. How old are you?"

"Seventeen, but my birthday is in a few weeks."

"Okay, let's say you're eighteen. You're almost a woman. If you're a woman, then you ain't a child. And, if you ain't a child, then that means that you have to start taking care of yourself now and start making better choices for your life. Stay out these places that you're going to. Get away from these low-life, two-bit punks like Jinkins. Have some pride in yourself, girl. Have some pride. What would your daddy say to you if he'd seen you like this? Would he want to see his baby prostituting herself for a piece of garbage like Jink?"

Without waiting for a reply, he turned around and walked away. Gwen watched as he disappeared into the distance before she slowly walked up the three flights of stairs up to her apartment.

Pat-a-cake, pat-a-cake, baker's man/
Bake me a cake as fast as you can/
Pat it and shape it and mark it with a "B"/
And bake it in an oven for my baby and me!

Patty cake, patty cake, baker's man/
Bake me a cake as fast as you can/
Roll it up, roll it up
And, throw it in a pan
Patty cake, patty cake, baker's man!

****

Gwen kicked off her sandals immediately and started to undress as she walked towards the bathroom. There was only one. It was outside at the end of the hall, which had to be shared by three different tenants.

She turned on the water. The sound of that first splash on that scuffed, porcelain tub sounded like the first notes of a symphony.

She waited nearly minutes before the water turned manageably warm and inviting. Moments after stepping into the shower, the small puddle at her feet became cloudy, billowing brownish-grey clouds. She looked up only to prevent the shampoo that she was pouring on her dry, tangled and messy hair, to not pour out in the tub. She massaged the liquid soap into a rich lather while trying to pull out the knots of matted patches of mud that had glued together.

As she lifted her face to the water raining out of that pipe, the music of the shower beating against her slowly disappeared as the voice of the old man played back in her head.

"Young lady, I've been seeing you around... now look at you!"

Gwen leaned out of the shower and reached for the bottle of shampoo that she placed back on the bathroom sink. She squeezed a quarter-sized drop in her hand while remembering the bottle cap that was on the sidewalk when she stepped out of the taxi.

"We see your types every year."

Reaching through her thick, soapy hair massaging her roots, she stood still for a second. 'What did he mean, *"We see your types every year?"* What type am I? He doesn't know me.'
"What are you doing with a hoodlum like Jink? Boy-o' boy....! Can't you see what you're getting yourself into?"

Gwen lowered her head in front of the nozzle and allowed the water to wash the backside of her hair. She raised her head and let the water pulse against her forehead.
"Don't just stand there looking like a dummy. Don't you have anything to say for yourself?"

She reached for the bar of soap and began to lather it in her hand before she rubbed circles all over her face. She lifted her washcloth from the hot water knob and gently wiped the soap from her face. After wringing the cloth, she rubbed the bar of soap against it and began to wash her body starting with her neck and working her way down.

"Get away from these low life, two-bit punks... boy-o-boy... a hard head makes a soft behind!"

When she reached behind her, the words low-life and two-bit-punks brought her back to the evening before when she stood outside the club and saw Robert Lee and Wally ogling her rear. What was I thinking? What was I trying to prove? Did I really want guys like that to come on to me? I wasn't dressing like a ho. Who do they think I am?

"Stay outta those places!" The words of the old man shook her.

Gwen saw the damage done to her bare feet as she sat down in the tub. She drew her legs into her thighs to examine her feet. The downpour of water erased the blood-stained scratches that went from the tip of her toes all the way to her ankles, not to forget the gash that cut through her jeans. She sat there and began to cry. It was then, at that moment, when she remembered the safety of her grandmother's house in Madisonvillle, Kentucky. And, the reminiscent aromas of her mother's cup of coffee and the plate of fatback bacon and biscuit that would be waiting for her at her grandmother's house. 'What am I doing here? What am I doing in places like these nightclubs? Or, walking past people in booths leaning down and inhaling some white powder or seeing two men and a woman in the bathroom stall? What am I thinking,' Gwen thought to herself.

She knew this was not how people behaved in her small town.

"What are you doing with Jink... he's a hoodlum!"

'No! She thought to herself. No, my Jink's no hoodlum. That's my man! He no hoodlum! You don't know him like I do. You have no right to say those things about him. Gwen held her head in her hands and started to cry. That's my man you're talking about. He's not a bad guy! You got him all wrong!'

She slowly stood up and turned off the water. She wrapped herself in her towel before she reached under the sink to find the bottle of Comet. She liberally shook patches of the powder all over the tub and cleaned it thoroughly before she headed back to her room.

When she opened her apartment's door, she felt a mixture of relief and sorrow. She told herself she would never let that happen to her again. Usually, she'd put on her day clothes and get something to eat, but she felt her bed calling her. She laid down with her bath towel still wrapped around her. 'Why,' she thought to herself, 'why would anyone want to hurt me? I'm a nice person. I come from a good family. I'm not a ho.'

She turned from laying on her side to laying on her back. Her mind went blank as she looked at the cracked, off-white ceiling paint. Her eyes became heavy, and as she drifted off she heard the old man's voice once more,

"What would your daddy say if he saw you like this?"

four

"A hard head..." his voice echoed. "A hard head leaves a sore behind... You're a stubborn girl... We've seen your kind before.... Get out of those places... Why are you just standing there like a dummy?"

Gwen drifted off to sleep
****

Right side, left side, right side; her head turned back and forth. Her lips quivered at first, but slowly she began to see herself sitting on the top step at her grandmother Cecil's house in Madisonville. It was vaguely familiar, but Gwen didn't realize that she wasn't laying down in her bed in Charleston.

She looked around and noticed a middle-aged man in a powder blue, two-piece suit with a matching straw hat, holding the hand of a pretty little girl with four long ponytails and white barrettes clipped to them. She wore a white chiffon dress, ankle-length white socks and white shoes. It didn't feel like a Sunday, but they were certainly dressed as if they were going to church.

Gwen watched as they approached and followed their steps as they walked by her. Gwen would have followed their travel had it not been for Cecil, who had just come outside and sat down on the step next to her.

"Granny..."
"Yes, dear. What's the matter?"
"Granny... can I ask you a question?"
"Dear, you can ask me anything. You know you can."
"Granny, do you know where my daddy is?"

Cecil was quiet for a moment. She wondered how she would answer this question without it getting back to Lila Mae. Cecil was well aware of where Gwen's father was as his parents kept her abreast, but not Lila Mae. And they made Cecil keep these updates a secret.

"Why do you ask?"
"I just do, no reason," Gwen said, with a look of puzzlement on her face.

Cecil knew that when Gwen wanted to know something, she wouldn't stop until she was satisfied with the answer that made the most sense to her. Cecil also knew that if Gwen somehow found out that she was aware of her father's whereabouts all this time, she would completely lose Gwen's trust.

"Well child, your daddy works far, far away from here. Why all of a sudden you'd want to know about that?"

Gwen stared at her slippers, feeling ashamed that her long suppressed feelings were now interpreted as ungratefulness.

"Granny, can I see him?"

Cecil remained quiet as she hoped that this day wouldn't come until much later. She brushed her hands on her apron. She got up and walked back into the house without looking at Gwen.

*

Cecil and Lila Mae packed a big lunch for Gwen. Cecil also checked to make certain that her bag had plenty of clean panties for the next couple of days. Still, she worried that her granddaughter's sassiness may cause her to get into trouble.

A week later, Cecil and Lila Mae put Gwen on the seven a.m. Greyhound bus. Gwen, sitting next to another little girl, pulled down the window and waved goodbye to them. She could see Lila sobbing on Cecil's shoulder as the bus drove off. She sat back down in her chair and didn't say anything to her new seatmate for almost an hour.

After a long, quiet ride, Gwen's seatmate decided to break the silence and offer Gwen a stick of her new unopened pack of gum. From that moment on, Gwen and her new friend talked and laughed for hours. It didn't seem as if six hours had passed when the bus pulled into the station. As they disembarked, the little girl turned back to Gwen and screamed out, "Goodbye, Gwen." At that moment, a man of average height, maybe five foot five with broad shoulders and a muscular chest and a burnt umber complexion yelled from a distance,

"My baby! My baby!"

Gwen walked to this stranger slowly with both of her bags in tow and stood in front of him. Silent, and not knowing how to respond to the cheerful man who loudly proclaimed,

"Look at you! My baby! You are so beautiful! You look just

like your mother!"

Gwen smiled but didn't respond. Charles Collins took her bags and put it in the back trunk. He talked incessantly, not stopping until they reached the house.

"Chuck," as he was known to his suburban neighbors, lived in a two-story house with Mary Rorer. They had a three-bedroom home, with one room on the main floor, and two full bedrooms upstairs. Upon entering the home, Gwen saw Mary, an older lady maybe twenty to twenty-five years older than her father. She was at least a foot taller than him but walked with a limp. Gwen didn't know if the limping was because of an accident or because of her heavier weight.

Gwen stood and looked around the living room. She smiled to herself because her father was still talking from the time they left the bus stop. A moment later, Mary in her soft tone and polite gesture said to Gwen,

   "Would you like to see your room, dear?"
   "Yes, ma'am. Thank you."
   "Oh, I'm sorry, Gwen. Charles said. "This is Mary. She'll show you to your room."

Charles said as he smiled at Gwen.

"Miss Mary" as Gwen would call her, took one bag and left the other bag with Gwen. Mary climbed a few steps, caught her breath and then labored up the rest of the stairs. Once at the top, she held on to the railing for a few short moments before walking Gwen to the room a few feet away.

When the bedroom door opened: it looked just like the rest of the house in Gwen's mind. Everything is neat and in order. It was immaculate as if no one dared walk into the room. Gwen couldn't help to think about how much time was put into keeping this room clean. She recognized that she most like got her compulsiveness for neatness from her father.

"Well, Miss Gwen, I'll call you for supper after I'm finished cooking."
"Thank you, ma'am."
"It'll only be a little while. I've been preparing for your arrival all morning and I know you're hungry from the long bus ride."

Mary turned around and walked out closing the door behind her gently.

Gwen opened the bedroom window, first out of necessity but then as the warm breeze came drifting in, she began to remember why she wanted to come here. Why hadn't he come to see her? And why had he abandoned her mother, Lila Mae?

Dinner was ready a short time later. It was maybe fifteen minutes since Mary had left. She heard her name being called from downstairs. Gwen hurriedly took off her shoes and put on her bedroom slippers, as she felt like she had a lot to do in her two-and-a-half-day trip. She recognized that Charles wasn't going to make it any easier on her.

When Gwen got downstairs, she was lead to the sound of Charles and Mary's voices in the kitchen. Charles sat at the end of a table, and Mary had her apron on taking out dishes from the oven and putting them on the counter. She spooned out black beans and rice from the pot into a serving dish. Gwen was about to ask if she could help when Charles said,

"That's okay. Mary will handle it. Come here; let me see you. I haven't seen you in so long. Look at you. You're as beautiful as your mother. You know, your mother has always been a beautiful woman. And, you are as beautiful as her, you know that?"

Gwen said nothing but looked away hoping to see something to hold her attention.

"How's school?"
"Fine."
"Fine? That's it, just fine?"

Charles cocked his head trying to read in her silence what was apparent on her face. Is she shy or is it that she doesn't like me, he surmised. Why hasn't she addressed me? Charles stared at Gwen, but she refused to look at him directly for more than a couple of seconds at a time, but mostly looking down at her hands that were folded on her lap.

Charles repositioned himself on his seat and removed his wallet from his back pocket. He removed a bill from his billfold and put it on the table in front of Gwen.

"This is yours if you call me Daddy!" Gwen didn't dare raise her hand, but she stared for a moment at the bill. She never saw a $50 bill before. "Go ahead and take it. It's yours, but you have to call me 'Daddy!'"

Gwen looked at Charles, but a mixture of confusion, anger and disappointment were intermingling in her mind all at once. This was a stronger emotion than the feeling of knowing that she could have those pair of high-heeled shoes she saw in a department store back in Madisonville, in her possession. She could actually see and feel them on her feet. But, she also had to imagine where she'd hide them, in her room at home under her bed maybe, from Cecil and Lila Mae?

Gwen looked at the money and made a little sigh. She rested her chin on top of her hands that laid on the table and stared endlessly at her fingernails. "That's alright, baby. I know it must be tough, I know you still got questions you want answered before you do that. And, I respect that. I'll give you all the time you need."

After dinner, Gwen went upstairs and took a shower before going back to her bedroom. She laid on the bed and thought about that moment at the dinner table. She reflected on Mary and had endless thoughts. 'Was she happy? Would momma be in the same type of relationship as her if he had stayed? Would they have lived here? Why did he leave us,' she thought? 'Why did you do this to momma? Why? Why did you do this to us? Why? Why did you do this to me? Why me? Why?'

*
****

5

Laura prided herself on being physically fit and could have easily played varsity if she were in high school, but walking up three flights of stairs to visit Gwen was an entirely different thing.

As she reached the top of the stairs, she heard a faint noise but didn't know where it was coming from. She stood still, hoping to discern what it was, but the sound came and went through the hallway like a spirit. A few careful steps later and a raised hand, she decided to press her ear against the door instead. She couldn't make out what it was, but it sounded like Gwen, it's just that the voice was a bit groggy. She readjusted herself hoping to hear better. On the other side of the door, she heard a raised voice say *"Why! Why me!"* The room fell silent again. Laura spoke gently,

"Gwen?"

She heard no response. Then as she was about to knock again, she heard, *"Why did you do that to us?"* Silence, again.

"Gwen, is that you?" Laura said as she held her hand back from knocking once again.

Laura stood back a foot away, then carefully knocked twice.

"Gwen...are you there? "

After a moment of silence, she gently knocked again, twice,

"Gwen...Gwen, honey, are you okay?"

Laura gently turned the knob on the door, hoping that it was unlocked. The knob turned to its end, and the door slowly parted. Laura first peeked through the sliver of an opening where the light was coming in.

"Gwen...Gwen... it's me, Laura. Are you all right? I'm coming in now, okay?"

There was no answer for a moment until she heard the voice clearer,

"Don't touch me! You don't know me!"

Laura pushed the door a little bit wider but very slowly in case something threatening was happening.

"Gwen... Gwen... it's me, Laura."

The door was now halfway open, but Laura could see most of the apartment from the spot at the doorway, where she stood. Laura saw what looked like Gwen on her bed but no one else around. Gwen was tossing and turning. Laura crept toward her, not knowing if someone, especially Jink, was standing outside of her field of vision. When it appeared that no one else was in the apartment, Laura walked a little faster to Gwen's bed.

She saw Gwen's bath towel in a bunch off to the side, and she noticed all the scrapes, scratches and bruises that were all over Gwen's body. From head to toe and everyplace in between, there was not one area that wasn't bruised; even Gwen's face had long jagged scratch marks across her cheeks.

She stooped down and gently cradled Gwen's face in her hands, Gwen was still mumbling and pounding her clenched fists against the mattress. Laura leaned over and hugged Gwen. It was just a moment when she felt Gwen move under her hug. She looked at Gwen and smiled, but Gwen seeing the image of her father, Charles, said, *"No, I won't call you, 'Daddy'... Get away from me! I hate you!"*

Laura then cupped Gwen's face and looked at her without saying a word. Gwen stared at this face, which dissolved from Charles' to Laura. She looked around and saw her dresser, her dining room table, and her radio, and she realized she wasn't in Kentucky. She was home. And, it was Laura who was standing right in front of her. She rubbed her eyes and felt her heart rate and breathing go down.

Laura helped Gwen to sit up, and as Gwen began to remember how she got here, she realized she was naked. As she leaned up, she noticed her bunched up towel on the floor, so she grabbed the sheet and pulled it up to cover her chest. Laura returned with a glass of water.

"What happened to you, Gwen?"

As Gwen was about to bend over and grab her towel from the floor, she said,

"Two guys... I know them from Candyman's... they tried to rape me, and they threatened to kill me."

"What! What are you talking about, Gwen!"

Raising up her arms, pointing to her cheeks and the scrapes on her inner thighs, Gwen said,

"I got these running away from them. I got away by running through this field about maybe 2:30 or 3:00 o'clock in the morning. It was right after Candyman's had closed and I didn't have enough money to get home. I had spent most of my money on drinks and food there... and a couple of other clubs I went to last night."

"Well, I don't know of any field by Candyman's, where were you?"

Laura said with a bit of confusion in her tone.

"I went out clubbing' last night to forget about Jink because I realized that I spend too much time alone looking at these four walls after work. So, I was there dancing and having a good time, jumping from club to club all night. And maybe I had a bit too much to drink too. Anyway, I got away, and this elderly lady helped me to get a cab back."

Laura stood in front of her with her arms folded. Gwen could read the disappointment on her face. Laura had told her countless times that she needed to stay away from these places, and more so for keeping Jink's company.

"Laura, if you're going to preach, don't! What I need is a friend right now. I already feel bad enough as it is."

"I'm not here to condemn you. I just came by to say, hello. I hadn't heard from you since Jink left and your phone's not working," Laura said with a bit of defensiveness in her voice.

"I know you haven't heard from me," Gwen said, "but I felt like I was all alone. That's why I went out last night. Maybe I wasn't ready for that yet?"

Gwen turned to her phone and lifted up the receiver and heard no dial tone.

"I don't know why my phone's not working. I gotta check it out tomorrow when I go back to work."
"Are you hungry," Laura said as she adjusted the strap of her shoulder bag. "Maybe we can get something to eat?"
"I don't have any money. I gave everything I had to the cab driver. I'll have to go to the bank tomorrow when it opens up."
"I have some money. Let's put some clothes on and get some... fish and chips? How about that?" Laura said with a smile.

six

It's true when they say, "All politics is local." That's never been truer here in West Virginia.

Here in West Virginia, no one exemplified or exerted more political influence than Senator Robert Byrd. True to his name, Robert Byrd, born Cornelius Calvin Sale, Jr., was many things to many people. He was a "good ole' boy," an intellectual, a car salesman, a priest, your late night drinking buddy, and even a segregationist, but he was never regarded as a bad politician.

He was anything he needed to be to get elected, get re-elected and to get funding for projects that his constituents wanted. It wasn't unusual to see him in a pair of jeans drinking moonshine or on a porch eating strips of fatback bacon and corn bread while telling colorful jokes. You could also find him wearing the most expensive tailored suits money could buy.

As with every successful politician, Senator Byrd had a gift for gab. For many of those outside of West Virginia, Senator Byrd was both a contradiction and an enigma.

He railed against the Civil Rights Movement and Dr. Martin Luther King but in impoverished areas, there was no better friend. He always found monies to support educational and vocational training for minority groups and for the less fortunate.

He was a chameleon with whom everyone benefitted from. The Job Corps Centers in West Virginia was one of the biggest beneficiaries of his legislations.

The Job Corps program is an educational and training center that is directed toward young men and women who come from impoverished environments. The re-institution of this program in 1963 was open to young people from the age of 16 to 19. For individuals who showed promise, the Job Corps offered their "Advanced Training School," which extended their education another five years depending on the discipline they elected to study. Acceptance into these selected courses was only based on the recommendation of the primary school's directors' decision.

Originally introduced in 1933 as a part of President Franklin Roosevelt's "War On Poverty" program, that program was called the "Civilian Conservation Corps." It was only for boys, and it was primarily an agricultural endeavor. That program had a cap of three hundred thousand applicants.

By the time the CCC ceased in 1942 during the States involvement in World War II, the organization had helped more than three million young men.

While the idea of high unemployment for young white men was high during the Great Depression, it was substantially higher for minorities as a whole. Two leading African-American scholars W.E.B Dubois and Booker T. Washington argued about how to address the inequality for jobs that were not offered to minorities who were living in the same conditions as the poor white neighbor counterparts.

Both men looked at the vast potential that young African Americans could offer, but essentially offered different paths. DuBois considered a liberal, intellectual education. It was the gateway to the middle class exposing African American youth to research, entrepreneurship, mentorship and teaching. Washington, on the other hand, exhorted politicians and business leaders to "drop down their buckets" in the vast sea of day laborers. Washington was more concerned with satisfying the abundant needed for unskilled, uneducated labor to do farming and agricultural work.

It was some twenty years later while assessing the same persistent problem that Sargent Shriver re-envisioned the CCC as an amalgam of DuBois intellectual foundation and Washington's pragmatic appeasement. With this idea worked out in his head but needing funding, Shriver believed that a revised CCC would work as a means of satisfying two legitimate needs for all young people, including women. The Job Corps would be a place where they operated a dual educational system, which offered such diverse programs like nursing and clerical work besides hospitality-related courses.

He sent it to President Lyndon Johnson for consideration.

Today, there are more than one hundred and twenty Job Corps locations throughout the United States and since its inception; Job Corps has trained more than ten million young men and women to enter into the job field.

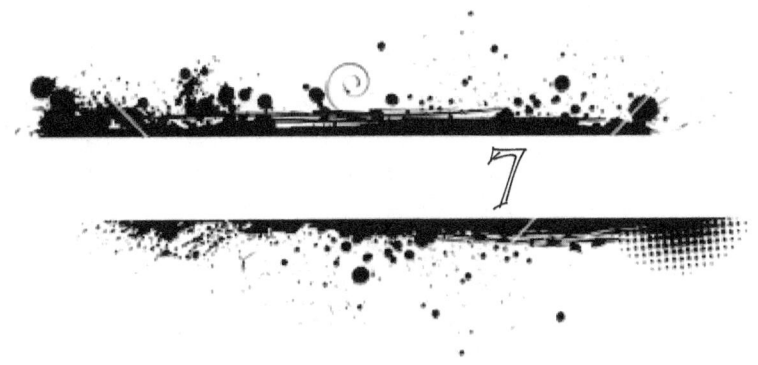

7

Monday mornings were always the busiest time of the week at the phone company. Work that should have been and could have been done on Friday afternoon became a Monday morning emergency.

It's been a lively few days since the morning rush started at 7:30 a.m. A walk around the room tells a compelling story to visitors.

There are mostly women employed here, with the notable mention of "Mister Raymond," a tall, slender and clean-shaven, straight haired man in his mid-30's. Although some people thought Raymond relaxed or chemically treated his hair, it was naturally long and straight. He answered those inquiries by stating that he's half black, half Indian. On occasion, just to fit in, Raymond would blow dry his hair and pick it out into an Afro, but every time the air conditioning went out, Raymond's home-styled Afro would frizz out.

Raymond got along very well with almost everyone because he was designated the office's fashion consultant. No woman worth her paycheck would dare to cross Raymond after he pronounced his opinion on how well she was dressed at that moment. To do so would earn her a lecture on his credentials as a "well-sought after advisor to the stars." It was his duty; he reminded the room to make sure they were educated in the delicate art of wardrobe etiquette. "Something that these women", he'd casually state from time to time, "Had no apparent or instinctual capacity for."

If a woman were to forget her place and respond to his not-so-indirect approach, she would risk him writing her name in his dreaded, powder blue, "Demerit Book." And THAT was a no-no.

Gwen always earned herself a passing grade. Raymond always loved her choice of heels with a coordinating set. He would tell Gwen that if she ever became famous that he'd quit his job at the phone company and work for her as her clothing and make-up consultant. The only thing he chided Gwen about was her ample posterior. As he'd tell her, "Men don't like all that extra stuff back there, it's time to clean out the garage!" Gwen always smiled at his comments, wanting to say to him, "If you only knew!"

****

This particular Monday was a bit different. Jink wasn't around and because of her activities just 48 hours before; she didn't feel comfortable being in the middle of the room where all of the other agents could easily see her. So, Gwen decided to sit in front near the door. She thought it would be easier to run out of the room quickly if her situation became unbearable for her.

She wore a lot more makeup than usual. This included layer and layer of flesh-tone foundation, moisturizing creams and eyebrow pencils to create a new layer of skin over her own to hide the still-visible bruises.

Sitting near the entrance of the office meant she had to sit near Dania and Marilyn; two middle-aged women who've worked for the phone company for more than twenty-years. These women, among several other quieter workers, remembered how hard it was at the onset, especially for anyone without the right connections to get a job in downtown Charleston. That goes double with the phone company. Yet, here they were considered "Job Corps Whores" getting more freebies from the government. They were particularly upset with the mayor, while the state legislature began to place the Job Corps graduates in well-respected and well-sought after positions in supervisory roles.

For many young and older women, whether they were single, married or divorced, these ladies from the Job Corps schools were nothing more than lowlife trash and whores. No one ever questioned the veracity of the tales that were often told and retold. Everyone just assumed that their clothes came off easier than a stick of Wrigley's Chewing gum. And Gwen, associating with a local vagrant like Jink, didn't win her any friends at the telephone company either.

****

Gwen loved working at the phone company. It was the one place where she felt instant gratification after helping customers with their needs. As she was attending to some calls, she could overhear Marilyn and Dania directing their criticisms in her direction without having to turn to face them.

"Hmmm, I wonder why we have someone new sitting by us today? The last time I checked THAT seat was always opened for Miss Lane to use when she needed to. Do you know anything about that girl?" Marilyn said as she turned to Dania for confirmation.

Dania, with her lips curled and her arms crossed, wearing the standard one-ear headpiece said,

"Child, I don't know what's going on here, seems like they let all kinds of folk up in this place. It's bad enough they bring these skanks off the street and give them a job, but they got a lot of nerve coming whenever they want, going wherever they want and doing whatever they feel like," Dania said.

While Marilyn nodded in agreement to Dania's comments, she turned to Gwen, but quickly forgot why when she noticed some discoloration on Gwen's face. She turned back to Dania and said,

"D, you see this! You see this girl's face? Girl, go ahead and take a look."

Dania leaned over but this time lifted up her reading glasses and leaned in,

"Mmm hmm, girl I see what you're saying. She done look like she got into a fight with some alley cats and lost. I bet you she was trying to steal one of their men. And I bet after they finished whoopin' her ass, they chased her raggedy self out of the alley."

Marilyn lifted up her glasses to get a better view as well, despite the fact that Gwen was less than a foot away.

"Look at her," Marilyn said turning back to Dania. "She doesn't even have her makeup on right. Who taught her how to do makeup? Oh, no! I can't look at this. This is making my stomach sick. I was just about to get up and get some coffee, but now I just gotta take two Excedrin."

Dania, shaking her head,

"Yuck, I feel so dirty."

Gwen continued answering calls without turning around to respond to the insults. She knew that the people on the other end of her line didn't know or cared how she looked, they just needed her and that's what Gwen kept reminding herself.

The switchboards around the room began to light up like lights on a Christmas tree, and before she knew it, Marilyn and Dania were busy answering calls again. It was at this moment that Gwen felt a tap on her shoulder. She looked up and there standing beside her was Kaye Lane, the department supervisor.

"Gwen, I need to talk to you. Just take a break for a few minutes. I need to have a few words with you out in the hallway, and I also have someone on my private line who needs to speak to you when we're done."

Kaye looked down at her new black patent pumps before raising up her square, plastic glasses to speak to Gwen. Kaye was an intelligent woman whom was deeply devoted to her work and her family. She prided herself on dressing conservatively with little to no makeup. She always wore a sweater and reminded some of the workers of a librarian.

She was well aware that many of her operators were jealous of her success. It wasn't as Dania and Marilyn had surmised many years before when they all started out at the same time that either one of them and not Kaye who would get the promotion and become the department supervisor. Nor, was it Kaye's proficient use of correct grammar and soft-spoken demeanor was a deliberate attempt to get attention but it was exactly as the motto that was written on the sign that hung above her desk said: "Persistance Overcomes Resistance.

She shifted her reading glasses down her nose slightly but looked at Gwen solemnly.

"Gwen... I have a few things to discuss with you, and I need your full cooperation."

"Yes, Miss Lane. Did I do anything wrong?"

"No, not exactly. Your work performance is outstanding. You're punctual, and all of the right people see the work that you do and are impressed with you. This has more to do with your life outside the office here."

"I don't understand?" Gwen said with a puzzled look on her face.

"Gwen," Kaye said as she flipped through the stack of papers she held in her hand. "I have a bill here for.... for $500. Ahh, here it is! This is from the accounts receivable department. If you look at the top, it'll show you the total charges and this right here and all of those lines are a list of charges that have been made against your account."

"$500! How...? I mean that's not possible. I've never..." Gwen said as she tiptoed to see the bills in Kaye's hand.

"Well, apparently you have a bill of more than $100 and that includes several pages of collect calls. Have a look at them," Kaye said as she straighten out the papers and handed them to Gwen. "Now, I'm not much older than you and I know what it means to be in love, but Gwen, we all are aware that you've been keeping company with a man who has a bad reputation. You know exactly who I'm talking about. I know his name is Jink," Kay said to a silent Gwen.

She paused for a moment before she continued.

"Look, you're young, but you need to know people like that can bring you down. I'm also aware that he was arrested recently and is serving his time overseas. There are quite a few collect calls from his house to Germany, and they're applying those credit charges to your account."

"So, I'm on the hook for those calls?"

"Yes, I'm afraid you are. I'm afraid to tell you Gwen, that you have to pay this debt by the end of next week or your employment here at the phone company will be terminated."

"So, you're going to fire me because someone used my credit to make collect calls?"

"Look, Gwen, all I'm saying is that the company, not me, the company has these rules in place. If it were up to me, things would be different."

Gwen looked at her, then looked at the many lines printed on those pages and shook her head.

"So what am I gonna do now, Miss Lane? I can't lose my job. I've got nowhere else to go."

"Number one, I suggest that you find new friends and number two, maybe you can borrow the money and pay back a little at a time until your debt has been satisfied."

Kaye noticed that Gwen was starting to cry as she thumbed through all of the papers.

"Listen, I know I'm not supposed to do this, but I'm only doing this because I know what it's like. I had a boyfriend a long time ago that nobody approved of too, but I just had to be with him no matter what. There's a man on line 5 in my office. It doesn't show up on the switchboard circuit in the call center. Any calls from a high-security location will automatically come directly to me. I'll give you five minutes to say what you need to say to him, and I don't expect to hear any whispers around the office that I'm letting anyone use my phone for personal reasons. Is that understood, Gwen?"

"Yes, Miss Lane. Thank you so very much. I really appreciate it."

Gwen walked quickly to Miss Lang's office and sat in front of a beautiful phone she never laid eyes on before. There, flashing next to a light button was the number five. She lifted up the receiver and pressed the button. Gwen held the phone with a bit of trepidation.

"Hello?"
"Gwen, is that you?"
"Jink?"
"How come you had me waiting on this line so long, don't you know that I got a time limit? And, what's with your phone? I keep calling and I get no answer."
"Jink, my phone got cut off. They told me that this morning. They say I owe $500 for collect calls and charges. They think it's you and your family that's been using my phone line credit. That ain't right, is it?"
"Oh, so I'm the blame why your phone got cut off? How do I know you're not out there with another guy? You been sleeping around on me? I ain't been out of the country long enough for my coffee to get cold and here you are in bed with another guy."
"Jink...Jink... wait a minute. Hold on, let me explain. The phone company has records of calls from your mother's house or your sister's house...and someone's been telling the operator my account number. All I know is, somebody's been using my credit and if I can't pay this bill by next week, I'll be out of a job."
"Look, don't you even worry about a thing. You forgot who I am? Who am I?"
"Jink...my man?"
"Your man is right. Now what I need you to do is get yourself together and stop being a crybaby. It's time you put on your big-girl panties and remember who I am. Anyways, I called to tell you

that I'll be home soon."

"Soon!"

"Soon. I just need to get a few things done here and I'll be home, hopefully, to stay, but you know how that go!"

The moment Jink finished that last remark, almost on cue, Gwen heard a tap on the glass to the office. It was Kaye tapping her watch then she walked off.

"Jink, I gotta go. Are you okay?"

"Yeah, I'm okay. Why would you think otherwise? Ain't nothing here holding me down. Just keep it together and I'll be home soon to take care of my baby."

"Okay, Jink. Bye."

Gwen sat at her desk all day, not taking a lunch break. She didn't seem to recognize any of the calls coming through on her line because the thought of Jink coming back so soon possessed her thoughts. She also found herself worried about the bill and her job situation too. What about her rent? Jink? The telephone bill? It was like a merry-go-round that wouldn't stop. All of her thoughts ended with her living out on the street. How was she going to get this money?

Work was over, and all the employees filed out of the room. But Gwen didn't get up until everyone had walked out. She sat on the bench in the hallway and dropped her head down into her lap and just wept. Suddenly, she felt the bench move by the weight of someone sitting on it. When she looked up, there was a woman she had seen around the building occasionally but never had the opportunity to meet.

"Hi, Gwen! You look like you could use a friend right now."

Gwen wiped her eyes,

"Have we met before?"
"No, not really but I know who you are. I've noticed you since you first started, and my supervisor told me once that you were one of the star operators that we have."

The woman adjusted her bag and extended a hand,

"Hi, my name is Louisiana, but some people call me 'Lou-Lou'!' You don't mind me sitting next to you, do you?"
"No," Gwen said while wiping her eyes. "That's okay. I was just getting up."
"Are you okay. I've never seen you like this."
"No, I'm good."

As Lou-Lou saw the mascara stain on a piece of tissue that Gwen was folding, she put her hand on Gwen's lap.

"Gwen, whatever it is that you're going through, I want you to know that God's gotta plan for you. He's got a plan for each of us. Are you a Christian?"
"Well, I grew up in the church and I sang in the choir, but that was awhile ago."
"It doesn't matter how long ago that was, God still has his arms out waiting for you. All you have to do is go back to Him and He'll make everything alright."
"Thank you, Lou-Lou. That's very kind of you."
"You know what, I sing in the choir at my church too, and my husband is a deacon there. Here, take my card and if you feel up to it, I'd like to invite you to my church. And even if you want to sing with the choir, I sure they'd be more than happy to have you sit in with them,"

Gwen looked at Lou-Lou for a second and realized that she had let

her spiritual life lapse. She looked at the card that Lou-Lou gave her and recognized that she was just given an opportunity to sing, something that has always been her biggest dream.
Here was a chance to sharpen her skills.

eight

Finally. Finally, Friday had come and not a moment too soon. The week felt longer than usual: the pain of Monday morning's news was still fresh in Gwen's mind but didn't feel as scary.

Gwen walked straight home except for a brief stop by the corner store to pick up a few items for dinner. After her shower, she sat on the top steps outside of her door, just like she used to sit on the top step of the porch at her grandmother Cecil's house.

As she slowly sipped from a can of soda she brought with her, she just sat and watched people walk up and down the street: singles, couples, children, parents, window shoppers, and even a kid riding on a skateboard and snatching a woman's handbag.

Somewhere between all of the mundane and criminal moments that played out before her curious eyes, Gwen noticed a man running from beneath her view, downstairs through parked cars to a vehicle in front of her building.

Gwen stared at the face of the young guy but because of the

distance, couldn't make out exactly who this face actually looked like. Yet, she recognized his walk and the slight limp he had. She took another sip of soda while looking at the chipped step underneath her feet when she remembered that she passed him one day last night.

****

She was just leaving her apartment and walking down the stairs when she saw him from a distance standing in front of the neighbor's door. He reached into his pockets and brought out a hand full of bills. Then, a woman's arm extended out of the apartment and handed him a packet of marijuana cigarettes. He grabbed a few and stuffed them in any available pocket he could.

As Gwen reached the landing before walking out into the foyer, he heard her footsteps and stopped what he was doing. He quickly turned around and stared at her with such intensity that actually scared her. Gwen turned away quickly and walked out of the building. As she remembers that day, while walking away from that building, she also recalled promising herself that she'd really find out what was going on in that apartment.

****

'That's a great idea,' Gwen thought as she got up to put on her sandals. She hadn't been high in a while since before Jink left. She loved the rush she got when she inhaled. She could immediately feel a tingling in her head, a little lightheadedness and the slight burn in her throat just thinking about it. She knew her worries would drift away for at least 45 minutes. Gwen knew that's just what she needed.

Gwen walked down the stairs with a $10 bill stuffed in her back pocket. She reached the door and held her hand for a second questioning whether or not to proceed. She could hear noises inside, but couldn't make out what was going on. She hesitated slightly before she let her fists hit the door. 'Eh, what the heck', she thought, 'she could only say, no, right?'

She knocked.

Suddenly, the noises on the other side of the door ceased. Gwen knocked again, only this time a bit softer. She heard movement coming toward the door. Instinctively, Gwen took a step back.

"What can I do for you?" A voice said behind the door.

Gwen looked around just to make sure it wasn't someone else the voice was talking to.

"Hi... uhmm, can I ask you a question?"
"What's it about?"

Feeling frustrated, Gwen said,

"Is it okay if you opened the door, I don't like talking to wood?"

A moment passed, the lock was unlatched and the door opened just ajar, slowly. Just enough to for the chain links to pull.

"Hi...uhm, can I buy some weed from you? I'd like $10 worth."
"Weed! You mean, Weed, the drug?" The voice said with surprise.
"Yes!" Gwen said with anticipation in her voice.
"I'm sorry, but I don't know what you're talking about. We don't do that stuff 'round here. Who would tell you that? You need to go someplace else with that." The woman's gruff voice was firm.
"But…"

Gwen was about to say what she saw.

"Go on, now. Get outta here before I call the police."
"Okay, my name is Gwen and I live upstairs. I don't mean to bother you but I really need some right now. Do you know where I can get some?"

Gwen reached into her back pocket and grabbed the crumpled bill. She unraveled it and showed it to the woman.

"See, I got money!"

There was no response to Gwen's comment.

"Okay, I don't mind sharing it with you. I got nothing to do and we could just share it and talk?"

The woman didn't respond and closed the door in front of Gwen. Gwen shoved the bill in her back pocket and turned to go back upstairs when she heard the door open again. The woman came out and walked past Gwen; she sat on the steps overlooking the street.

With her back facing Gwen, she raised her arm and motioned for Gwen to come over. As Gwen approached her, the woman opened her hand. In it was a dime bag full of weed. Gwen immediately reached for the bag when the woman said,

"Mmm...mmm...Where's the money?"
"Oh! I'm so sorry!"

Gwen snatched the bill from her pocket and with one motion put the bill in front of the woman's face.

"I'm sorry, but..."

"My name is Miss Delores."

"Oh, Delores, well-"

"No. I didn't say my name is Delores. I said my name is 'Miss Delores.' After I get to know you... if I want to get to know you...you can call me, 'Miss D' for short."

"I'm sorry, Miss Delores."

As she was saying this, she noticed that Miss Delores had opened the package and had spread out a small white piece of paper. She took pinches of leaves and piled them up about three-quarters of an inch high in a long row from the top of the paper to the bottom. She rolled the paper up and had a long, thick, pencil-length cigarette. She rested the cigarette barely on the tip of her bottom lip while she leaned down and pulled out a lighter from her pocket. She lit the tip of it and took a couple of puffs before the cigarette caught fire. Soon after, the hallway was filled with a faint-colored mist that drifted from one end of the hallway to the other.

"You that girl from upstairs, huh?" Delores said as she passed Gwen the joint.

"Yes!"

"You're not with that short guy anymore, with the fur coat and the brown and white Stacey Adams?"

"Oh, you mean Jink?" Gwen inhaled and passed the joint to Delores.

Delores nodded. Then taking a drag from the joint, Gwen noticed Delores' deep inhale almost burned through the entire cigarette in one try.

"That's my man."
"Where's he now?"

Gwen lowered her head,

"It's a long story and I don't wanna talk about it."

Delores looked at Gwen from the corner of her eyes as Gwen took the last drag from the joint, and exhaled,

"What do you do girl?"
"Me? Oh, I work for the phone company in customer service. I'm one of the operators and..."
"Okay, I know what you do. I see you and Jink around and I thought you did something else."
"Something else? Something else, like what?"
"Oh, he didn't tell you what he does for a living?"
"He told me he works the late shift and he does something with checking his traps."
"Checking his traps! That's all he told you?"

Delores shook her and laughed to herself.

"Check his traps. My, my, my. Girl, you got a lot to learn. There's one born every minute."

With that, Delores slapped her legs and got up and walked to her door without saying anything to Gwen. Gwen sat there for a moment after Delores closed her door and wondered what she meant by that.

9

The following week had started and the due date for Gwen's overdue phone bill was just three days away; still, Gwen had no resource available to get the money. She still hoped something would open up for her.

It was the end of day, Wednesday. As Gwen and her co-workers headed out to leave the building, they came to the door to see heavy rains and winds beating against the door. The downpour was so strong that no one could see the other side of the street. One of the ladies pressed her face against the glass hoping to see if there was an easy path to her car that was parked across the street. She shook her head and said something to the lady next to her.

Raymond squeezed in between the women to see for himself.

"Oh, no. This can't be happening. I just got my hair done. Do any one of you have a spare rain cap; I need to tie my hair down? Do you know how long it took for me to blow dry this into an Afro this morning? You have no idea!"

Gwen shook her head slowly as she looked at the lightning flash across the Charleston skyline. 'How am I gonna get home,' she thought to herself. One of her friends who was standing in front of her, wrapped herself in a plastic bag and ran out the front door.

"Gwen, are you okay? Can I give you a lift someplace?"

Gwen turned around to see whom it was who was talking to her when she saw Lou-Lou.

"Gwen, can I give you a ride someplace?" Lou-Lou repeated.

Gwen looked at the doorway and the heavy rains beating against the glass.

"I live at The Lang Apartments. Do you know where that is?"
"Yes, I do but I'm headed in the opposite direction. Can I drop you off at the bus stop nearby, because I'm late? I have to pick up my daughter from school." Lou-Lou said with a bit of worry on her face.
"Sure, that's no problem," Gwen said.

The two women braced themselves then made a dash a few yards away to Lou-Lou's car. The women drove a few blocks to the nearest bus stop going in Gwen's direction.

"Gwen, I won't leave you out here in the rain before your bus comes. My daughter can wait a few more minutes for me. My husband lives in Delaware and we try to visit him a couple of times a year. That's how I spend my vacation. We're going to see him in a few weeks."
"Oh, Delaware. I heard a lot about it. I would so love to go," Gwen said innocently.
"Well, if we have enough room, maybe you can come with us," Lou-Lou said. "Your accent? Gwen, where are you from

because you don't sound like you're from around here."

"I'm from Chicago," Gwen said as she wiped her face with a rag from her bag. "I've lived there all my life but we moved around a lot, so I can't say that I'm from one town specifically."

Lou-Lou titled her head,

"I never met anyone from Chicago before. Is it nice? I hear that it gets very cold and windy?"
"You don't know the half of it. The winters feel like you are in Siberia!" Gwen said without blinking an eyelash.

Lou-Lou suddenly saw the headlights of Gwen's bus in her rearview mirror.

"Gwen, I think this is your bus."

Gwen turned and saw the number on the bus,

"Yes, that's my bus. Thank you so much, Lou-Lou. I really appreciate it. I'll see you tomorrow, okay? Thanks for the ride and yes, I'd love to visit Delaware if that's possible."
"Let's see. Be safe now, ya' hear?" Lou-Lou said to Gwen just before the passenger side door closed.

****

The ride home was unusually bumpy, but Gwen had other things on her mind. She had roughly 48 hours to resolve this issue with the phone company or she'd be out of a job.

The rain was still heavy and looking through the windshield didn't yield a better view, even with the windshield wipers going at full speed. She peered at the signs as they were just above the top of the bus and when her stop finally came, Gwen anxiously pulled on the chord several times. The driver slowed to a stop before turning around to see who was constantly ringing the bell.

"Sorry!" Gwen said with a smile as she draped a piece of plastic over her and hugging her bag next to her. She jumped across a puddle before hitting the sidewalk. She grabbed her small damp rag she used to wipe her face and quickly brushed off some of the dirt that spotted her sleeves.

She stood up and fixed her bag as a new gust of wind brought a fresh new batch of heavy rain. She ran to the sidewalk and found herself in the doorway of Rite-Aid drugstore. There was no hiding place from this rain even with the store's awning hanging overhead, but it gave Gwen a chance to adjust herself.

"Excuse me, Miss. Do you have a dollar? I haven't eaten all day."

Gwen turned around and saw a woman huddled on the floor on the other side of the doorway.

"I'm sorry, did you say something?"
"Do you have a dollar? I'm hungry."
"Yes, I think I do," Gwen said as she started to pick coins scattered at the bottom of her purse. "Okay, here you go. Why are you just sitting here? Do you need bus fare to go home?"
"I'm not going home... my father just died and my younger sister lives with my auntie. I just need to get away to think about what I'm gonna do now," the woman said as she accepted the money from Gwen.

Gwen readjusted her wrap as the rain was now attacking her from several different directions. She looked down at the woman curled up and drenched.

"Why don't you come with me? You can stay the night with me and tomorrow you can make plans on where you want to go. You okay with that?"

"Oh, God bless you. You don't have to do this, but I really appreciate it. Thank you, so very much," the woman said as she struggled to get to her feet.

Gwen gave her a hand up and they both walked the few blocks to Gwen's building. As they approached The Lang Apartments, a young teenage girl ran quickly ahead of them into the doorway. When Gwen and the woman came to the entrance, they saw ripples of red drops that lead through the doors and up the stairs.

Gwen and the stranger tiptoed carefully around the bloody stream. As they approached the second floor, they saw the young girl banging on Miss Delores' door. The bloodied footprints lead up to the door but Gwen couldn't tell where exactly the blood was coming from. The young woman's dress was drenched and her legs were coated down to her feet.

Gwen turned to the stranger, "Wait here; I'll be right back!" Gwen rested her bag down next to the stairs and walked around the footprints to see Miss Delores' door. She peeked inside but didn't see Dolly, however, she did see a room straight ahead and down the long narrow hallway. At the end of the hallway, the door was wide open.

As Gwen took a look from the distance, she partially saw a bed facing the door and the young girl laying face up on the bed. Her feet were lifted up high, pressed against the wall. Gwen thought the young girl must have believed the bleeding would stop if it staying inside her.

Just then, a lady came out from an adjacent room and noticed the trail of blood on the carpet that went past her room. She crept to the side until she reached the room with the open door. She noticed the girl's bloodied feet pressed firmly against the wall. But, when she stood over the girl and saw the blood all over the bed, she screamed.

Gwen leaned back quickly as not to be seen by the woman who went running out of the room.

On the other side of the door, Gwen heard this panicked woman's frantic call to the ER. Gwen leaned forward again and saw the young girl getting up from the bed holding her stomach. She stumbled down the hall and turned into the bathroom. The woman on the phone rested the receiver on a table and ran to the bathroom. Gwen wanted to go inside but feared whomever was there would not like to have a stranger intrude in their space. A moment later, Gwen heard the knob on the bathroom door turn and the woman ran out. She ran toward the area where the phone was.

"Hello... yes, I'm just with her.... no, she's still bleeding. Something came out of her; we don't know what it was... I don't know if she's sick or not...she just bleeding... it's coming from her vagina...that's all I know. Are you coming or not? She's bleeding what more do you want me to say to you... we're at The Lang Apartments. I know... I know jus' tell them to hurry. I don't want her to bleed to death."

Gwen tiptoed away. When she got back to the stairs, she picked up her bags and heard the ER coming through the lobby.

"Miss, let's go. I don't wanna be standing here when they come."

Gwen and the woman quickly went to her apartment.

Once settled in, Gwen gave the stranger a towel and soap. She showed her where the bathroom but waited at the stairwell a little while before going back inside. She could barely hear the voices of the ER, although the walkie-talkies were turned up to their highest volume. She heard their heavy footsteps leaving from Delores' door.

Gwen ran back to her apartment and looked out the window. She saw the young woman being carried out on a gurney. The drive through the heavy rain and thunder was slow, but Gwen said a silent prayer for the young girl as the truck disappeared into the darkness.

ten

The night had been a restless one for Gwen. She tossed and turned all night. Dreams and nightmares were indistinguishable. She saw herself homeless and sleeping in a dumpster. In another dream, a covered plate was put before her in a restaurant and when she lifted the tin cover, she saw a decomposing rat with flies swarming everywhere. In another, she saw Jink, who looked so much older and thinner. Gone were his furs and minks, he was now wearing ripped and dingy jeans and a torn shirt that hung over his emaciated chest. His gaunt eyes looked cloudy as if he had cataracts. He stood shouting through a broken window in an upstairs apartment of an abandoned building. He was yelling something to someone, but Gwen couldn't hear him. Then, he jumped.

Gwen got up in the middle of the night to get a glass of water. She stepped over the stranger who was sleeping on the floor wrapped up in blankets. She looked at the woman as she sat on her bed and wondered what this woman's story was. Then Gwen realized that she hadn't asked this woman what her name is. The woman hadn't asked Gwen, either. Anyway, Gwen thought, she'll be on her merry way today and that'll be the end of it. Besides, I did a good deed.

****

Gwen rolled herself into a bundle and pulled the covers over her. It was a bit cold that night, but more importantly, she was able to minimize breathing in the foul vapors that were living in that woman's clothes.

Gwen quickly drifted off to sleep only to find herself standing in the hallway a few feet away from Delores' door. The trail of blood that leads from the steps into Delores' apartment seemed to be moving like choppy waves over an ocean. As if it were beckoning Gwen to follow it. Gwen walked slowly around the areas that didn't have splashes of blood on it until she got to the front door.

Delores' apartment door was open, but no one seemed to be inside. The blood trail it went all the way down the hallway and into the bedroom straight ahead.

A few moments later, the door slowly opened. Gwen saw the bed against the wall, as she remembered it from a few hours before. Someone on the bed started to move. Gwen realized it was the young woman who was bleeding.

The impulse to follow was getting stronger in Gwen until she relented. She carefully walked inside, being cautious not to step into any blood and not to look into any room to the right or to the left. But with every little step, her peripheral vision only saw the side walls. They were closing in on her as she walked closer and closer to the room. As she approached the doorway, she could see the young woman, but not her face. She saw her laying on the bed wearing a soaked nightgown, scraped knees and bruised feet that were pressed hard against the wall. The nightgown, with its yellow teddy bear print, seemed familiar to Gwen but she couldn't place where she saw it before. 'Did I have one just like this?' Gwen wondered. Her mind was cloudy.

The young woman slowly turned over with her head hung down. Gwen walked over hoping to ask how she was feeling, when the young woman lifted up her face, Gwen saw herself. Gwen shook her head in disbelief and was about to scream when the young woman vanished and all that was left beside the blood-soaked bed was the stained footprints on the wall.

****

Gwen felt something tug at her shoulder. She opened her eyes and the image of her guest slowly came into focus.

"Are you alright?" You were just screaming. I think you were having a nightmare."

Gwen looked around and she was lying on the bed with nothing covering her; all of her blankets were on the floor and her pillows were wet with perspiration.

"Yes...uhh...I'm good. I'm good."

The woman grabbed the empty glass from her nightstand and walked to the kitchen for more water. The woman looked over her shoulder,

"Can I get you anything to eat? Do you want me to make some scrambled eggs and toast? You want coffee?"

Gwen slowly sat up and slid her feet into her slippers. She heard the woman but she also remembered the many voices that haunted her in her dreams still playing back in her head.

"No, thank you. I gotta get ready for work. I'm sorry but I forgot to ask you your name," Gwen said as she wiped her mouth and unpinned her hair.

"Oh, I'm sorry, my name is Teresa, but my friends call me, Terri."

"Terri, okay! My name's Gwen. Nice to know you. Terri, I don't mean to rush you but I have to leave in a few minutes after I come out of the shower. I'm gonna leave my key so when you're done getting your things together, you can lock the door and leave the key underneath the mat. Okay?"

"Sure," Terri said. "I just need to make a few phone calls and I'll be on my way."

"My phone's not working. You'll have to go to the phone booth at the corner. Here..."

Gwen walked over to counter where her bag was. She opened her purse and maneuvered through a bunch of coins.

"Here's three dimes, that should get you some quality time."

"Alright. I owe you so much for last night. Thank you again Gwen, for everything. God bless you.

****

Gwen left her apartment about twenty minutes later, saying her last goodbye's to Terri as she ran for the bus.

As she was on her way, she knew she needed to ask for an extension on her debt. She still hadn't figured out how she was going to get the money. The fear of her losing her job and not being able to pay her rent made her freeze in her boots.

The day came and went. It was all a blur. Gwen wasn't even sure she was giving the customers the right information. The time had come for her to leave for the day and she needed to resolve the issue with the phone company.

As she worked up the nerve to see her supervisor, she turned to push out her chair and she looked up and saw Miss Lane, standing before her. Their eyes met but neither said anything for a moment.

"Gwen?"
"Yes, ma'am."
"I've been authorized to give you an extension of one week if you didn't have enough time to get the money."

Gwen began to cry.

"I know how these things are and believe me, I feel for you. But if you don't have the money by next Friday, I'll be forced to let you go."
"Thank you so much, Miss Lane. I really appreciate all that you're doing for me." Gwen wiped her eyes and the drool from her nose with her sleeve. "I promise I'll do my best to get you the money."
"I know you will and I'm sorry about all of this but I don't have any choice. This is just the way it is until the company makes a change."

Gwen walked out with gratitude and headed home. She got off the bus a couple blocks away from her apartment, feeling the weight lifted off her shoulders. That was until she realized she'd be in the same predicament next week if she didn't get the money.

****

'The worries can wait until after the weekend,' she thought. It was her time to put her feet up and just enjoy the day. As she approached her building, she started digging in her bag looking for her key. 'Where's my key? Did I leave it at work by my terminal? Could I have left it in the bathroom? Did I take it out on the bus?' Gwen searched her mind frantically until she remembered that she left it with Terri.

She ran up the stairs with renewed energy, not knowing if this woman was really a thief and she would be left with an empty apartment. 'I'm such an idiot. I should have made her leave at the same time.' Gwen thought to herself as she reached the second floor.

As she turned to climb the last flight of stairs, she looked over to Miss Delores' apartment. There were women standing there wearing very, very short shorts and big high heeled boots, some even past the knees. One even wore a bright green fake fur jacket. What are they doing there? 'Ugh, I wouldn't be caught dead in that? Raymond would have a field day with them.'

As she started upstairs, she heard a familiar voice addressing them. She noticed the women going in their bags and handing Delores wads of money. 'Where did they get all that money? They must work for some kind of Italian designer to have all that money.'

Gwen made it to the top of steps and took a deep breath. She gathered herself and walked slowly to her door when she smelled spaghetti coming from her apartment. She took a step back and very gently lifted up the mat hoping to see her key there. It wasn't.

Gwen stood up and placed her hand on the doorknob and twisted it. The door opened and Gwen peeked in, leaning her body against the door. When the door was opened wide enough for Gwen to see the whole room, there in front of the stove straining the spaghetti was Terri.

"Terri.... what are you doing? I thought you were trying to get a ride to live with your relatives?
"I'm sorry, Gwen. Things didn't quite work out the way I planned. I don't have a place to stay. Nobody wants me."
"Terri, I let you stay here last night because I didn't want to see you sleep in the rain, but you can't live here. My lease is for only one person. What if the landlord finds out?"
"Gwen, I understand that but this is not permanent. I just need a place to stay until I can get on my feet and then I'm gone."

Gwen didn't respond. She put her bag down on the nightstand next to her bed. She pondered. She loved the fact that she didn't have to cook, and having her here would make her feel less lonely for Jink.

"Okay, Terri, I can give you a few weeks, but that's it. Do you understand?"

Terri turned around with a big smile on her face and a plate of spaghetti and meatballs for Gwen. Terri walked it over to Gwen and even placed a napkin-wrapped fork on the tray next to her plate. Gwen was hungry but she had a lot on her mind. She kept thinking about the young girl who was bleeding last night. So, Gwen slipped her feet into her slippers and walked past Terri into the hallway and down the stairs.

Gwen knocked on Delores' door with a confidence that only a friend could have. Gwen knocked again. Then she heard some footsteps approaching the door. Delores opened the door and stood there with a blank expression on her face.

"Can I help you?"

Gwen smiled and said,

"Hi, De-! Oops, I mean, Hi Miss Delores. I just came by to say hi and I wanted to let you know that I enjoyed our conversation the other day. Wanna smoke some weed and talk, 'cause I had some kinda week...I wanna tell you!"

"Excuse me, Gwen, but I think you misunderstood what that meant the other day. You and I are not friends. You're just some young, naive girl who has no idea what world she's living in. Now, if you'll excuse me, I've got business to attend to."

"Wait, wait, Miss Delores. Ok, Ok... I saw a young girl last night come into your place. Just tell me if she is alright? I just want to know if she's okay."

"She's doing fine. She just had a miscarriage, that's all. It happens all the time. It's no big deal. Now, if you'll excuse me."

"Wait, wait, what do you mean it happens all the time. What was she doing to cause her to have a miscarriage?"

"Boy, you are some nosey little something, aren't you? Look, I'm gonna invite you in because I've got to return this call. One of the girls will fill you in, but you can't stay long."

Delores opened her apartment door wide to let Gwen in. She walked in and saw Delores quickly pick back up the phone call that she was resuming. Miss Delores pointed to one of the women inside the living room, which was located immediately to the right when you came in. As a couple of the women pointed to themselves, Delores snapped her fingers and pointed to the tall, beautiful one with long, flowing black hair. She had a face that resembled a liking to Lola Falana.

The woman came over and asked Gwen what she wanted to know. Before Gwen could recall what she wanted to know, there was a knock on the door right behind her. Gwen turned around and opened it. A stocky man with a bright brown mustache and beard came in. He had tattoos on his underarm but they were too covered for Gwen to make out what they were.

Delores got off the phone and walked toward the man, bumping Gwen out of her way.

"Arthur, how's it going? You're looking as handsome and as strong as ever. You make me feel weak in my knees. Did you know you have that effect over women?"

The man smiled at Gwen but answered Delores,

"I've been told that."

Then he walked around Gwen and touched the lapel on her uniform.

"*What's this pin for darling?*" He said in his slow southern drawl.
"Oh, that's my one-year pin. I got it..."

Delores touched Gwen on the shoulder,

"Never mind. Now, don't you have somewhere to go?" looking sternly at Gwen with Arthur at her back.
"Oh, yes, I'm gonna go now."
"Now, wait just a minute there, young lady. You don't have to go so fast. I've never seen the likes of you in here before. Are you new?"

Delores grabbed Arthur's hand away from Gwen's,

"Arthie, she's visiting she doesn't work here. Besides, you wanted to see to April because she has a very tight..."

"Oh, yeah. But, I like this one right here. You think we can change and I can see April another time?"

"No, Artie, April has been waiting for you all day. She's got a special surprise for you. She told me herself...she's gonna make you a very, very happy man. Now, you wouldn't want to disappoint April, now would you?"

"No, I reckon I wouldn't. But, you think I could have this one the next time?"

"I'll see about that, okay?"

"Okay, I'm a just go ahead a wait here in the living room until she's ready."

Arthur turns to Gwen,

"Bye, now, darling. Daddy's gonna take care of you next time. Daddy's gonna take real good care of you."

As Gwen looked to Delores, she felt a heavy swat on her behind. So much so, that his hand actually lifted Gwen off her feet about an inch or two. Delores grabbed Gwen by the arm and walked her to the door.

"It's time for you to go." Opening the door, "And, the next time you come here, I'm gonna put you to work."

"There's something mystical about this place." Daniel Boone and his small regiment surmised as they reached the border of Kentucky and Southwest Virginia surveying the land. The frontiersmen, especially Boone, had a reputation of knowing the ins and outs of hills and mountains, which were dominated by the Iroquois and The French Canadian settlers. They had been commissioned by Gov. Lord Dunmore to rescue members of his Kentucky delegation who were being held captive in 1774.

Seventeen years later, Boone and his family would briefly reside in what would be known as West Virginia. He briefly became a legislator in the pristine Kanawha County, now the capital of West Virginia.

****

Nestled underneath the Appalachian Mountains and bordered by Virginia in the southwest, Northwest Ohio, Pennsylvania and Maryland in the north and northeast, respectively, West Virginia declared its independence from Virginia during the American Civil

War and became a state in 1863.

Charleston, the largest city and capital of West Virginia was named in honor of the father of the general who bought the land. He called this new area, Charles Town. Eventually, the name became Charleston.

Meeting at the cross section of the Elk and Kanawha rivers, Charleston was the center of commerce for a number of industries for the past one hundred and fifty years. Early commercial industries operating in this area were salt, natural gas and wild game. Charleston was one of the first primary commercial salt distributors in the world.

It was also home to General George S. Patton I, of the Confederacy, who led a revolt against the Union with his Kanawha Riflemen during the early stages of the Civil War. He was killed at the Battle of Winchester. His grandson, George S. Patton, Jr. would go on to be one of the WWII, greatest military strategists.

Other industries formed after the salt industry became saturated. The river ways enabled trade between northern and southern settlements. The capital also became home to utilities such as coal and electricity, the state's municipalities, a medical center and one of the state's marquis universities. Charleston is also home to the first brick street laid in the world. Summers Street was completed on October 23, 1863.

Metro Charleston, like every other city, is a collection of people, places and ideas: a melting pot of beliefs about what the American Dream should be.

Downtown Charleston was, indeed, a maze of streets beginning with Quarrier Street, the main artery in the southernmost part of the city. Quarrier Street went east and west... and to complicate matters, places that were acceptable were right next door to that which was forbidden. The Job Corps center was directly facing the notorious, XXX-rated, Lyric Theater.

There were a few streets that were alright to travel on during certain hours of the day, but after a particular time, workers, shoppers and school children would be replaced with street walkers, purse snatchers, drug peddlers and those desiring certain entertainment.

While it was not uncommon to see unlawful activity happen sporadically during the daytime, most of those who'd participate in these enterprises would congregate in bars and juke joints up and down the three main streets of Capital, Summers and Court, which all ran parallel to each other. However, the street that held sway among the city's matrix of vagrants was the infamous Court Street.

Court Street was known after working hours for its blatant and unsupervised prostitution and illicit drug transactions. And it was here, in the center of Charleston, it's most inquired about destination where people who'd never interact with each other during the day, much less on the weekends and whose residences were as far apart as the directions on a map, would meet.

The city's government officials were not lost or blinded by this undercurrent of social activities. They renovated an abandoned hotel in favor of the country's newly initiated Job Corps Educational and Rehabilitation services program.

When Charleston welcomed Gwen and the other Job Corps girls to its new center, the government officials, defined the city by borders: a "Red Zone" as the directors of the Job Corps put it.

But the "Red Zone," the Corps told its students, was not just an imaginary geographical line representing the border of what was acceptable and disreputable, but also one that represented cultural and psychological boundaries.

If, for instance you were a "Job Corps Girl", you were distinguished as having low-income, coming from a 1-parent (or less) household. You were a minority and most likely a high school dropout. You had no ambition and desired none. And most disheartening, your motivation was to take advantage of the accomplishments that the civic leaders and city's residents worked and fought long years to earn.

"A Job Corps Whore," as Gwen and the other 300 girls who were students there would learn, is a designation placed upon them by the city's residents. And with that title came the expectation that they'd drop out of the Corps and find work servicing the unfulfilled needs of people who came out at night.

It was usual for the Corps girls to be verbally and physically assaulted by the city's residents. Even just walking down the street, they could be profaned on the mere suspicion that one of them may have their attention on someone's husband, boyfriend or son.

These were the presuppositions, which the Corps girls had to work under.

twelve

The alarm went off at 7:30 a.m., but it was only after Gwen turned over and hit the top of the small radio that she realized it was Sunday. She normally had the radio set to wake her up during the week, but not on the weekends. Her job during the early morning hours of the weekend was to sleep. And, sleep long, hard and peacefully.

Almost ten minutes had passed before she was fully awake. She desperately tried her hardest to recapture her sleep, but she found herself staring at the ceiling. Her mind began to drift off to when she used to wake up this early on Sundays, a long time ago.

Her mother and her grandmother Cecil would wake Gwen and her brother Michael up early on Sunday mornings to get ready for church. It was part of the fabric of their existence. Church on Sundays and church on Wednesday nights were mandatory, like school, like death and like taxes, except she'd have to wait a few years before she could work legally.

Church rituals were the same each and every service. Only after having to wait until the grown folks stopped greeting each other in the lobby, was Gwen and Michael allowed to sit in the pews. Gwen and Michael always found fun when in church, whether it was tearing pieces of paper from the program and flicking them on top of people's hats, to sneaking under the pews to share jokes about which member looked most like what animal.

But if there was a saving grace for going to church for Gwen, it was during the song service. Singing wasn't the biggest part of the service for her; it was the only part.

When it was time for Praise and Worship to begin, it was Gwen's cue to perform for her audience around her. She always forgot she was a part of the audience herself, but when that first note came, it was like a door opening up to an open field with the sun shining down on it. This is where Gwen shined.

****

Gwen looked at the clock and remembered where she would be at that moment back in Madisonville. She felt homesick. For the first time in many years, she missed church. She wiped the tears from her eyes and remembered the church invitation she received from Lou Lou.

She sat in bed and went through her purse. She found the card with the information it. It read: First Baptist Church of Charleston 432 Shrewsbury Street. In front of Garnet High School. She nodded her head; she knew the area. Gwen looked back at the clock. She thought she could make the last service, but she would need to get ready quickly.

Its red brick facade teased of its opulence inside. When Gwen walked in, she immediately thought to herself that she was nowhere close to Madisonville. The beautifully high vaulted ceilings draped the massive church's length. The pews were situated in two long rows of oak wood seating covered with plush velour fabric. Gwen knew it was a long time since anyone here sat in foldaway chairs. However, the thing that stood out the most was how crowded it was.

Gwen arrived at church uncomfortably late, considering she was even later than the church's own "CP" members. She had an excuse though, she thought to herself as she made her way past the people who sat at the back; she was a guest.

Gwen looked around for Lou Lou throughout the course of the sermon but forgot that Lou Lou sang in the choir herself. Just before the end of the service, the pastor commented that a guest vocalist would sing a few songs with the choir to close out the service. As the guest vocalist began to sing, Gwen found herself singing the same song. She was hardly aware that the members around her took notice of her. She was oblivious to the fact that she sang just slightly lower the choir.

At the end of the three songs, church members around her extended a hug and thanked her for bringing tears to their eyes. Some even commented that she sang better than the choir's guest.

As Gwen was about to walk out, she saw Lou Lou dressed in her choir robe standing next to the exit door.

    "Now, you weren't going to leave without saying goodbye?" Lou Lou asked with a smile on her face.
    "Oh, my gosh! I didn't see you." Gwen said as she opened her arms for a hug. "Where were you?"

"Girl, I sit right over there next to the pole, but I saw you and we heard you from the stage. You have such a beautiful voice. You need to be a member here and sing with us!"

"I don't know about that," Gwen said. "Singing is all I've ever wanted to do. I was born to sing."

"Okay, you don't have to decide just yet. Can I give you a ride somewhere?"

"I was just going home. I was about to call a cab."

"Cab! No! I'm taking you home and that's the end of it."

*****

The church was relatively a short distance away by car, although it felt longer by taxi to Gwen. On the way, Lou Lou couldn't resist talking about visiting her husband who was in Delaware, when she noticed Gwen looking out of the window and silent. As she was nearing the apartment, she turned to Gwen,

"Is it him, you're thinking about?"

Gwen looked to her,

"I really miss Jink. My life doesn't feel complete without him."

"I got a great idea that'll take your mind off of him for awhile. Since you've never been to New Jersey, why don't you come with me? I could use the company and you can help me with the kids?"

"I would love to come, Lou Lou, but you know I'm about to lose my job. Don't you remember?"

"Oh! Oh, my! I forgot. I completely forgot. I was so excited to see you at church, I completely forgot. Dear, I'm sorry."

Lou Lou turned forward and slowly turned into a parking space almost in front of The Lang Apartments.

"I wish I could help you but my husband's away, he sends me what he can and I've got to do the rest myself. I just don't have it to spare."

"I'm not expecting anything from you, Lou Lou," Gwen said. "I can't afford to go and spend the little I have because I don't know when I'm going to find another job."

"I have a friend who works at the Holiday Inn a few blocks away from here. She cleans rooms and she says they're always looking for room staffing. You think you might be interested?"

"Yeah! I'll take anything. I'll even sweep the street if they want me to. I gotta eat and have a roof over my head," Gwen said with excitement.

"Okay, I'll see what I can do. I think it'll be easier for you getting in because of your experience with the phone company? Now, how about the trip? You think you can make it now?"

"If you're going, I'm there!" Gwen started laughing with joy at Lou Lou.

"Oh, my goodness, Gwen! I've got to meet someone in an hour, I almost forgot. Can we finalize this now? Can you help me with the kids on the trip? It'll be for three days. We leave on Friday and get back here on Sunday night. Does that work for you?"

"Yes, it does! Yes, it does indeed! I'm so excited Lou Lou. Girl, I tell ya, when I tell ya, when I tell ya. I've been wanting to go up to that area for a long time. I have an uncle who lives in Brooklyn. I might just call him when I get there."

"You sure can. Okay, I gotta go now. I'll see you on... what time Friday? Wait! Why don't you sleep over on Thursday, that way it'll be easier for us to leave on Friday?"

Gwen, standing outside the car but looking in, paused for a moment,

"Yeah, I think that'll be okay. Alright, I'll bring my bags to work

on Thursday and we can go to your house afterward."
Lou Lou started the car and back up again.

"That sounds like a plan. Okay, girl. God bless you and keep you safe until I see you at work tomorrow."
"Bye, Lou Lou!"

Gwen waved at her from the front steps of her apartment. As Lou Lou drove off, Gwen felt a burst of excitement. 'Finally,' she thought. 'Finally, she's going to get away from Charleston, at least for a few days.' Happiness was finally coming back her way and the prospects of another job offer made Gwen jump for joy.

Before she could turn around and walk through the door, a couple of random men crossed her path at the same time. Two men, both white, met her at the doorway. One was coming up the stairs behind her and the other was leaving out the door. She looked behind her at the man who was leaving the building and he waved goodbye to someone in Miss Delores' window.

Gwen was too excited to think about who those men were. It's about Delaware! She wanted to celebrate with a joint and maybe some quick girl-time chatter with her new buddy, Delores, if she was available.

The good news was too good to keep to herself.

13

Gwen couldn't wait to blurt out the good news. She opened her apartment door only to find Terri fast asleep across her bed. 'Never mind,' she thought, 'that'll free me to talk with Delores without having to repeat myself.'

Gwen grabbed some clean clothes from her chest of drawers and scoop up a pair of her two and a half-inch high-heel sandals with a bow design on front. She bought them awhile back but only wore them once when she went out with Jink. She closed the door quickly and ran down the stairs to Delores' apartment. She took a deep breath not wanting to get too excited about her plans.

She knocked on the door twice. The door opened up and a woman Gwen hadn't seen before answered it.

"Yes? What you here for?" she said.
"Hi, can you tell Miss Delores that Gwen, her friend from upstairs is here for her?"
"Okay, just a minute," the woman said as she slowly closed the door.

The door opened up a minute a later and Gwen saw Delores with the phone receiver wedged to her ear and the phone base in her hand. Delores motioned for Gwen to come in.

Gwen walked in and observed her surroundings. Delores' living room was to the right with a window that faced the street below it. To the left was a table with a telephone on it and behind it was a narrow hallway that led to a row of bedrooms. Although, she'd have guests to visit her girls, drug sales was a very small part of her operations, as Gwen would find out over time.

Gwen turned around when she heard the receiver replaced on the base.

"Yes, Gwen. How can I help you?" Delores sighed with a bit of frustration.
"Hey, Miss D! Wanna get high? I got some great news I wanna share with you!" Gwen said, with a grin from ear to ear.
"Gwen," Delores said taking a deep breath, "don't you see that I'm working? I have all these people here and you chose the busiest time of the week to bother me?"
"Oh, I'm sorry. I...I apologize. Okay, I'll come back another time," Gwen said as she turned to the door to leave.
"Wait!" Delores said, "I'm glad that you came over. I need a break. Thank you for considering me."

Gwen smiled,

"Miss D., can I have ten dollars worth of weed. That'll be enough for us, right?"

Delores smiled,

"Yes, I think that'll be enough. You know, I don't have many friends, only co-workers. You're one of the few that just come over just to talk. I like that about you. Okay, next time it's my treat."

Gwen searched her shorts and realized that she forgot her money.

"Miss D., I'll be right back. I have to go upstairs to get my money."

Before Gwen could make another step, a tall, white man stood at the door just about to knock. He was almost six and a half feet tall, and about two hundred and ten pounds. Blotches of acne surrounded his cheeks and he had dirty blond hair that was cut lower on the sides with a wave of locks that hung down over his forehead. He looked at Gwen for a moment, staring at her up and down, then he smiled,

"Excuse me, may I come in?"
"Sure, I was just leaving," Gwen said.
"No, you don't have to do that on my account. We haven't even met yet and you're already saying goodbye," the tall gentleman with the Southern accent said.

Gwen turned to Delores to see what she thought about such a comment. Delores looked back at Gwen and said,

"Gwen, please stay for a moment, I think I can use your help. We'll deal with that conversation later."

Delores looked that the gentleman and extended her hand,

"Jim, it's nice to see you again. We weren't expecting you, but Marlene is in the back finishing up with another friend. She'll be more than glad to know that you came by to see her."

Jim, or "Slim Jim," as the women of the house called him, behind his back, was a semi-regular. It was a description of him in height and weight. He was a referral from a client of his in the construction business who heard about Miss Delores' services and he became a regular afterwards.

That client of Jim's was a regular of Marlene's, but he re-committed himself to his wife after a debaucherous night of hard drinking and self-reflection. Jim was fascinated with the stories of the women here and Marlene's lack of inhibition in particular. Jim's visits and interludes have been happening about once or twice a month for the past several years now.

Jim shook Delores' hand and turned around to see the backside of Gwen. He rubbed his chin,

"I want to see Marlene but could I have her too?"
"Her, too?" Delores wondered for a second, looking at Gwen who was frozen by the suggestion. "Why, yes! Yes, you can but that'll be extra. You know that she would make her own money with another guy."

Jim smiled,

"How much extra?"

Delores looked at Gwen, then looked back at Jim.
"Double what you normally pay."
"Double," Jim frowned. "That's a lot. Is she that good?"

Delores answered with flinching,

"Let me say this: You'll be having twice the fun," then Delores leaned into him and lowered her head, "... and she never, ever experienced someone the likes of you before. I think you'll leave a very, very big impression on her."

"*Never?*" Jim said, smiling.

"Never," Delores said with a solemn look.
Delores looked over her shoulder as Marlene stood there in silence.

"Oh, here she is, your number one girl!"

Turning to Marlene, Delores put her hand on her shoulder and looked deep into Marlene's eyes,

"Now, Marlene, we have our very special friend here and he has a special request of us and I know you'll be on board with his idea. 'Jim...,' Delores turned to Jim with a smile, "Jim wants to be friends with you and Gwen. Can you show Gwen how we make our friends feel comfortable?"

"*Me and her?*" Marlene said.

"Yes, you and her. Remember how Jim has always been generous with us and has always returned to show his gratitude. Now we wouldn't want to disappoint him now, would we?"

"No, Miss D." Marlene turned to Jim, "*Jim, you know you're right at home here. We're never going to say, 'No.'*"

"Now, Marlene remember to take some of the towels and a water basin and escort Jim to the room. When you're finished, come back and take Gwen with you to get ready."

Delores looked at Jim,

"Jim, why don't we square away our affairs before you see the women."

"Okay, *Delores!*" Jim looked at Gwen as he was walking away, "... and Gwen, it's nice to meet you. You and I are going to have a lot of fun together."

Marlene walked with Jim to the room at the end of the hall. She first had to make certain that it wasn't occupied. After they walked out, Gwen approached Delores,

"Miss D., I can't do that. I have a boyfriend. I told you that before. I'm seeing Jink."

"I know what you told me, girl. But, I told you the last time you were here that I'm a business woman. That means, I'm about my business first and being a woman, second. Furthermore, I told you, if you come down here again, I'm gonna put you to work."

"Well, what about Jink? I don't want to do anything to upset him." Gwen said, in a moment of despair.

"Well, what about Jink? This is about business. This is about my money. This is about you getting paid. I'm not like your pimp boyfriend, Jink."

"Jink's no pimp. He's a fisherman," Gwen said.

"A fisherman! A fisherman selling a woman's trap. I bet you he's been keeping all of their money and only paying for their lodging." Delores said, with a raised voice. "Right here, in a few minutes, you will be able to make $50 for the next half hour of your time. You have a few friends like this and you can save up to have your own place."

"Miss D., why are accusing Jink of being a pimp?"

"Well, why don't you ask him yourself? He'll be here in a few days."

"WHAT! When? Where?" Gwen said as she tugged on Delores' arm, and pleaded with her to know.

"I don't know," Delores said, "one of my girls was having a drink in Candyman's and she overheard someone talking about it. She said Jink found a way to get a release from the service and he's working through the paperwork to get back soon," Delores said with her arms crossed.

Gwen started to pace in a circle.

"Now," Delores said, "are you going to help me...help us make this money or not. If you decide not to, I don't ever want to see your face darken my doorstep again."

At that moment, Marlene returned and stood in the doorway,

"*He's very excited to get Gwen.*"
"You see," Delores said to Gwen, "business is calling. Are you in or not? If you're not, get out of my place right now."
"I'm in," Gwen said softly.
"Okay, now you're thinking like a businesswoman. You don't ever let anyone tell you what you're worth. You decide! Now, Marlene's gonna show you the ropes. If you're good at it, we can make arrangements for you to have your own clients and your so-called boyfriend doesn't have to know."

Marlene tugged on Gwen's blouse and told her to follow. They walked to the room and stood in front of the door. Marlene peeked around Gwen's head to see if Miss Delores could see them talking.

"*Now, listen to me good. We only got a couple of minutes to get this plan right. This is my trick. You hear me?*" Marlene said to Gwen as she nodded. "*I know you don't know anything about this but this trick has got a lot of money, so what we're going to do is rob this fool of his money.*"
"Rob! Oh, my god, I can't do that! We're going to get caught!" Gwen said, with her hand over her mouth.
"*Just listen to me,*" Marlene said, "*I'm gonna do all the work. All you need to do is to grab his wallet from his pants and take the money out of it and put the wallet right back.*"

Gwen stood there in silence.

"You don't have to do this. You can go on and leave. I'll just tell Miss Delores that you changed your mind."

"Okay, how am I supposed to get his money when we're both supposed to be in bed?"

"That's easy. When we go inside, he's already going to be naked and laying down waiting for us. I'm going to undress first in front of him and get him started. Then you'll start to do a slow striptease. His pants are going to be on the floor in a bunch near the foot of the bed. When you start to take off your clothes, do one of those slow dances. Don't rush, and whatever you do, just drop your clothes on his pile."

"Oh, so when I'm finished and I'm picking up my clothes, I'll just go through his pants!"

"You're getting the hang of it. I thought it would take you a lot longer to get it."

It was no more than a minute after Marlene spoke to Gwen when they heard Jim call for Marlene. Marlene looked at Gwen without saying a word, but Gwen knew that look meant she couldn't mess up. She was trapped between Marlene and Miss Delores.

They walked into the room: Marlene first, then Gwen. Marlene smiled and slowly twirled as she made her way to the bed. She looked at Jim,

"You know I've been missing you, right?"
"That's what I like to hear. Daddy's came home today!"
"Yay! Daddy's home! Daddy's home. Daddy, I have something to tell you... I've been a bad girl since you left."
"A bad girl!"
"Yes, daddy, I've been a real, bad girl."
"Well, you know what happens to bad girls, don't you?"
"Yes, daddy, they get a spanking."
"Okay, get undressed. I told you every time you misbehave

there's gonna be punishment."
   "Yes, daddy."

Neither Jim nor Marlene took notice of Gwen who stood off to the side, surprised to see this performance start so soon. She walked very softly toward the foot of the bed where Jim's clothes were in a pile.

   "Gwen, I almost forgot you were here. Why don't you come and join us? Something tells me you were a bad girl, too!"

Marlene gave Gwen one quick look and then turned back to Jim,

   "Daddy, this is my friend Lynn, and she's very shy. She's sorry about what she did, but if it's okay with you, she's going to get ready over there. You can watch her if you want, or you can punish me for being a bad girl?"
   "You know, I think I'm capable of doing both at the same time, what you think about that, huh?"
   "My daddy can do anything he wants because he's the best daddy in the whole wide world!"

Gwen had her back to them as they were doing what they normally do each week. To hear the rumblings and the sounds of heavy breathing and moaning of the two people just mere inches away from her, reminded Gwen about that afternoon where she was trapped underneath her mother Lila Mae's bed as Lila Mae and her new husband had come home early and went right to bed. The sounds of the bed moving reminded her of those old spring coils underneath the bed that expanded and contracted while the old wood frame chipped and sprinkled down on her with every motion by the people above her.

This time, it was a little bit different. There was something about two people who weren't in love, as much as she could attribute her mother's relationship as love, yet were experiencing something so personal and intimate and not wanting it to have any kind of meaning other than a business transaction. It just felt weird to her.

Gwen couldn't tell where they were with all of this, but as she danced and started to remove her clothes, she dropped her outer clothes on top of Jim's pile and began to mix the clothes together with her feet.

Gwen had reached behind her and unhooked her bra when she heard Jim loudly moan. She looked around and saw his eyes closed but breathing very heavily. She glanced up to Marlene who was pointing very vigorously to the pile she was standing on.

Gwen quickly stooped down and dug through the pile until she felt Jim's dungarees. She pulled out his wallet, but not high enough for anyone to see it from their view. She slowly twisted the wallet and the currency started to show.

Gwen turned around to still see Jim recovering while Marlene laid on his chest. Gwen gave Marlene the thumbs up while Marlene smiled and returned the gesture.

A couple of minutes later, Jim sat up in the bed and raised his hands to the ceiling as he let out a big yawn. He walked over to his pile of clothes as Gwen was now buttoning her blouse.

"You ladies wore me out. I tell ya, I ain't young as I used to be, but you two keep me feeling young."

Jim grabbed his underwear and jeans and walked over to where the basin was and began to wash his face and dampened his hair.

Gwen and Marlene stood in silence after he put on his jeans and walked to the basin. He started to tap his back pocket where the wallet was then started to tap his front pockets. He looked at Marlene and said,

"For a minute there I thought I lost my garage keys, but I just remembered that I left them in the car!" He smiled as the ladies exhaled.
"Bye Jim. Am I going to see you next week?" Marlene said.
"You sure are. And, Gwen or Lynn, I want you to come back too. We still have some unfinished business to take care of."
"Yes, Mister Jim. I'll be here." Gwen said, trying not to engage in any lengthy conversation but needing to get out of the room as fast as possible.

Both women left the room as Jim was picking up his shirt and reaching for his shoes. They walked a few feet before Gwen found herself pulled in another room away from Miss Delores' view.

"You got all the money?" Marlene said with a worried look on her face.
"Yes? Well, I'm not sure, I was just grabbing what I saw. Here, you take it. I don't want any," Gwen said, terrified.

Marlene saw a nice wad of $10's, $20's and $50's in Gwen's hand. There was easily $500-$600 there, but Gwen couldn't be sure as Marlene riffled through that bundle like a cashier at the bank. Marlene pulled a few bills, folded it and handed it to Gwen,

"Here, this is yours. He'll be walking out in a minute after he says his goodbyes to Miss Delores. Then we can tell Miss Delores it was fun and thank her for the opportunity to make some money."
"I'm not really into to this for money. I...I..."

"Didn't Miss D. tell you this is a business? Jim is not my boyfriend. In fact, I don't like men. If I could, I'd be with a woman."

Gwen and Marlene waved him off as they stayed at the entrance of the bedroom door. Delores shook Jim's hand, smiled and waved him goodbye as she closed the front door. Delores then stuck her pointer finger out to Gwen and called her.

"Gwen, I want to tell you that Jim was very, very pleased with your performance. He wants to see you from time to time with Marlene and sometimes by yourself. Do you think you might be ready for that kind of arrangement?"

"I don't know Miss D. I mean, I just did this because I knew you'd be angry with me if I didn't. But, I don't know if I'm cut out for this kind of work."

"Okay, fair enough." Delores turned to the counter and picked up and envelope and gave it to Gwen. "Here, this is your share. He also gave you a tip ahead of time because he really wanted you to like him. I understand if you don't. This kind of work ain't for everyone."

Gwen took the envelope and walked out of Delores' apartment silently and without saying goodbye. On her way upstairs she heard voices on the other side of the steps. After walking up a few more, she leaned over the railing to see who it was. To her surprise, it was Terri and another woman sitting on the steps talking and laughing. She didn't bother to say anything. When she got to her apartment she felt glad that Terri had found someone other than herself to talk to.

Once inside her apartment, Gwen suddenly felt the weight of what just happened in the last few hours, to be too overwhelming to comprehend. She laid flat across the bed hoping to just sleep, but she couldn't. She wanted to cry but was too solemn. She unfolded the few bills that Marlene gave her and put it in the envelope that Delores gave her. A quick glance and a roundabout guess told her that she had at least $125 in hand. 'One hundred and twenty-five dollars? And all within three hours?' Gwen's thoughts came alive.

She had to get something to eat now because all of this was intriguing and overwhelming all at the same time. As she walked a few blocks to a small fish fry, she thought about how some people and some companies say that they value you, but don't show it. And to make matters worse, even if you're putting your best foot forward, you're still a second-class citizen, not worthy of their consideration.

On the other hand, many of these same people don't mind getting very personal with you... asking you to do things they would never allow you to even speak of just a few blocks over; and yet to engage with them in a behavior that they will readily admit is immoral, is rewarded with abundance and repeat business.

'What's wrong with this picture?' Gwen asked herself as she paid for her sandwich and made the trip back home.

fourteen

The day had finally come and Gwen couldn't wait to get up. Neighbors throwing out their garbage heard Gwen talking to herself in her apartment saying, "I'm going to Delaware! I'm going to Delaware! Na, na, na, na, naaah!" All they could do was just to shake their heads as they closed their apartment door.

Finally, Gwen thought as she folded some clothes to put in her new travel bag, she just picked up from Woolworth's the day before. Should I bring a sweater? Is it going to be cold? I hate the cold, she thought, but it will be all right since I'm leaving Charleston. Still, it was a bittersweet moment for Gwen because she would love to have Jink come with her. Delaware is near DC, so she was practically in New York! That was close enough to claim victory! All she had to do was finish the day at work and she'd be on vacation.

****

While at work, Gwen felt like it was Christmas Eve, and knew when she'd wake up the next morning, she'd have the gift she longed to have. Five o'clock couldn't come fast enough for her and although Gwen wore a watch, she was constantly looking up at the big clock in the room just to make certain that the time on her watch wasn't wrong.

Gwen glimpsed Lou Lou when she was walking into to work this morning, but could only wave to her from a distance. As the day came to an end, everyone waited in the corridor to file out and leave. Gwen's supervisor tapped her on the shoulder. She stood silent with her arms to her side. Gwen remained silent even when their eyes met.

"I'm sorry, Gwen," she said as she raised her hand with an envelope with it.

It was addressed to Gwen and it had her full name and address on it. Through the transparent window on the envelope, Gwen saw a pink paper folded with what looked like the image of a printed check on it.

"I had no choice. I fought to at least have you to finish out the week instead of on Wednesday."

Gwen slowly took the envelope from her hand and tears made their way down the sides of Gwen's face.

"I want you to know something. This happens all the time. You have no idea how many times I've been instructed to terminate an employee because they were behind on their phone bill. Gwen, look at me for second."

Gwen lifted her head up.

"If you need anything from me, please call me. I know a lot of influential people who may be able to help in one capacity or another... but you have to change your company. If a company thinks you're just some kind of ghettoish girl, they won't consider you for their company. You have to... no, you MUST have a better self-image, because if you don't, then you'll behave the same as everyone else, and become like the people you keep company with. And, you're much better than that."

The supervisor stood in front of Gwen for a moment, in silence, then turned around and walked away. As Gwen looked at the supervisor turn the corner and was completely out of her sight, Lou Lou walked right in sight. She saw Gwen standing by the door.

"Are you ready? Wait. Honey, have you been crying?" Lou Lou looked at Gwen red eyes and saw the envelope with the pink paper showing. "Oh, honey, everything's going to be alright. Remember the old saying, 'This too shall pass.'" She leaned in and gave Gwen a hug.

Gwen rested her head on Lou Lou's shoulder and wept.

"Gwen, honey, everything's going to be all right. Look on the bright side. You can start over fresh and do things the right way. Besides, in a few hours, we're going to be in Delaware! Isn't that going to be great!"

Gwen looked up and nodded.

"C'mon. Toughen up and be the strong woman you are. Nothing can get you down because you're in control-- the captain of your destiny. Right?"

"Yes," Gwen grumbled, "I'm good."

Lou Lou hugged Gwen's shoulder and walked her out of the lobby door of the phone company.

Gwen got in the car with Lou Lou as planned and headed to her house. The women walked up the stairs to Lou Lou's house carrying Gwen's bag and suitcase. Lou Lou opened the screened door to the enclosed patio and said hello to her parents, who were sitting in their rocking chairs looking out at the activities in the street.

"How are you, my dear," Lou Lou's father said to Gwen as she extended his frail hand for a shake.
"I'm doing fine, sir," Gwen said in response.
"Dear, it's nice to meet you. Lou Lou said she was bringing a friend over today before she left for work. She spoke very highly of you," Lou Lou's mother said to Gwen as she also extended her hand. "Would you like some tea, dear, or maybe some lemonade?"

Gwen smiled,

"Could I have a glass of lemonade?"

The old woman struggled a second to get up from her rocking chair and said,

"Oh, sure, dear."
"Momma, you don't have to do that. I'll get it for her. She's my guest," Lou Lou said.
"Now, Lou Lou, I'm halfway to the kitchen already," Lou Lou's mother said as she grabbed her cane that was leaning against the wall behind her.

Gwen and Lou Lou's parents talked for a couple of hours outside before continuing their conversation inside just before dinner. At around eight-thirty, Lou Lou's parents each told Gwen that they were going to turn in for the night. It was their time to take their medicine and retire for the evening. They each gave Gwen a big hugged and thanked her for coming over.

Gwen, thinking about the long trip in the morning, knocked on the children's room door. A little girl opened it revealing Lou Lou sitting on the bed with her children's books open. She was helping them with their homework.

"Excuse me, Lou Lou, I'm going to take a shower and turn in. We have a big day tomorrow."
"No, problem. I'm sorry again, that we don't have a spare room for you to sleep in. As you can see all of our rooms are taken. Are you sure that you don't mind sharing a bed with me?" Lou Lou said as she was looking at her son writing down an answer in his notebook.
"No, no. I'm good. I'm just excited about going!"

Lou Lou looked up at Gwen and smiled,

"So am I. I really miss my husband."

Gwen took a shower and folded all of her clothes neatly. She put them near the chair where Lou Lou had books and magazine's in a small pile. She looked at her things and smiled knowing in just a few hours she would be headed on a highway up to Delaware. Just before she cut off the light next to her side of the bed, she thought about what it would be like to surprise her uncle who lives in Brooklyn by calling him. How would momma react to such news? The thoughts invigorated her.

Some time had passed before Gwen drifted off to dreamland. The excitement of traveling was too much, so she often found herself too excited to fully sleep. The clock next to her side of the bed was broken, so she had no idea what time it was. She vaguely remembers when Lou Lou even came to bed.

******

Gwen looked up at the ceiling, her eyes were moving around the room's walls until they began to get heavy. Gwen finally drifted off into a sleep, a deep sleep. As the night went on, Gwen tossed and turned, scratching her face repeatedly, enough to break the skin and draw blood. Gwen tormented by her dreams, took her hands and did a pushing motion.

Finally, in a rage, she wakes up in a sweat shouting 'STOP, STOP, STOP!

Gwen opened her eyes and found herself turning her head back and forth, not able to breathe, but not able to make out in the dark room what it was. With every turn of her head, she felt the bristles of hair smothering her face. She lifted up her hands to shove whatever was in front of her, but as she moved her hands upwards, she felt the shape of legs.

Gwen pressed the back of her head into the pillow and moved herself up. When she looked up, she looked up and saw Lou Lou kneeling over her. Their eyes met and Lou Lou, with an expressionless face, crossed back over and laid on her side of the bed. Lou Lou reached behind her and grabbed the sheet to cover herself. Gwen laid still.

After a few minutes, Gwen got up slowly. She walked over to the chair where she had her slippers and slid her foot into them. She knew she had to get to the bathroom and how to get there, but her mind was completely numb. She quickly slipped out and made her way there. She turned on the light and walked to face the mirror. It took her a few minutes of staring at the image in front of her but slowly she came to back to herself.

In the mirror, Gwen saw her face dirtied with blood stains and scratches. Her face was soiled from her nose down to her neck. It took a minute before it registered to Gwen what had happened. She screamed uncontrollably.

Gwen didn't know what to do next, so out of reaction she looked at the hot and cold handles and turned the faucet on, all the way to the max. She looked back in the mirror and stared. She was disgusted by what she saw and couldn't look at herself in the mirror anymore, so she knelt down in front of the sink as the water ran down the drain and cried profusely.

She stayed there until she had enough strength to stand back up. She refused to look into the mirror this time until she had a chance to wash her face and pour water over her head. She kept her eyes closed and reached for the bar of soap, remembering that it sat on the dish. She rubbed and rubbed the wet bar of soap in her hair until she was convinced that she had enough to lather away everything.

It was at least fifteen minutes before she took some of the lather to wash her face. She felt for the faucet and carefully placed her head underneath the running water. The crimson stream slowly disappeared under the suds.

Gwen stood up, eyes reddened by the influx of water, but looked at herself anew, seeing only the remnant on her wet nightgown. She pulled off her clothes and threw it on the floor. Examining herself from her hair to her neck and her bosom, she was satisfied she was clean. She grabbed a towel that was on the rack and wrapped herself in it. She picked up the nightgown and balled it up with the stained part inside and walked out of the bathroom. Gwen changed her clothes, got her things and left Lou Lou's house.

Gwen gathered her things that were near a reading chair in Lou Lou's bedroom. In the darkness of the room, she slowly put on her street clothes and grabbed her luggage. Gwen slowly tiptoed out of the door. She turned around to look at the Lou Lou once more, but Lou Lou laid her head on the pillow looking away from her. Gwen couldn't tell if Lou Lou's eyes were open or not, but there was silence. The sound of the bedroom's doorknob squeaked when Gwen closed the door softly.

Gwen stopped and paused in front of the door where Lou Lou's parents slept, pondering whether to say goodbye. She declined and walked away. In a moment's time, she was in front of the house and was closing the gate behind her.

The walk home, what she was thinking and the time it took to get back to The Lang Apartments were all a blur. All she could remember was thinking, 'Why me? Why did Lou Lou do this to me? What did I do? What did I say to make her do this to me?'

As she walked towards her place, she kept the nightgown separate from the rest of her clothes. She had several thoughts about where to leave it. Should she have left it on the floor to remind Lou Lou of what she had done or left it on the floor just to embarrass her? She also thought about leaving it on the floor in the front room or in the kitchen garbage, so that her parents might see it and inquire about it. But, in the end, she wanted to discard the nightgown away from Lou Lou's home because like her mother, Lila Mae, she didn't want to miss the lesson that this pain had represented.

When she came near The Lang Apartments, she flung the bundle into the metal garbage container on the sidewalk, steps away from her place. She realized again that she assumed she could be taken care of by someone she trusted instead of plotting out her own path by her own means.

It was a message she was committed to mastering.

15

When Gwen reached to her bed it was 3:05 a.m., but she was wide awake. Gwen cried all night. She sat up in her bed with the brilliant light from the full moon shining down on her, but just cried. She felt a mixture of fear, intimidation and simply victimized. It was eerily familiar, but to what? She initially didn't make the connection, but she knew she couldn't go to sleep unless she traced the roots of her feelings.

She would cry and looked up in a dazed stare. Then she would cry again, but later regain her composure. Gwen was reliving that moment she saw Mr. Charlie put his hand up the little girl's dress who came to him for some candy. And the other moment when she was sitting on the toilet and a few feet away, some men were plotting to kidnap and kill her.

Each of these thoughts rotated inside of her head, constantly pushing their way to the front of her mind, vying for her attention. What was she doing to attract these things against her? It has to be more than the work of demons, but what was it exactly, she didn't know.

It was 6:35 a.m. when Gwen finally closed her eyes. It was also the first day she was unemployed. She laid her head back down: for the first time in years, she could actually stay in bed because there was no place she needed to be.

Gwen rolled out of bed almost an hour later. Her mind was clear, but she still felt queasy. She looked at the clothes on the floor and decided she needed to wash them right away. She heard a sound in the hallway, and when she cracked the door open, she heard the sound of people joyfully greeting each other. Gwen smiled and closed the door softly. Suddenly, she remembered that Jink was returning.

It took a couple of minutes of pacing around her apartment before she settled on going to Candyman's to see if someone there knew when Jink was arriving.

She put yesterday's work clothes in a bag, grabbed her handbag and walked out of the door to the laundromat. She told herself, as she put each garment into the washing machine, my yesterday is being washed away. Forty-five minutes later, Gwen grabbed an armful of clothes and threw them into the dryer.

She looked at the clothes as they tumbled over each other and wondered why things in her life never seemed to settle. Socks and jeans and other garments all intertwined and seemed to be constantly fighting to be noticed. She knew at some point, though, that things had to stop. But when?

There was a moment of vindication as she folded the dried clothes and put them into her small laundry bag. She flung her purse on her shoulder, grabbed the laundry bag and walked out of the Laundromat. She took a deep breath. Candyman's was only two blocks away.

**** ****

Gwen arrived just a few minutes after Candyman's opened for the day at 10 a.m. She was taken aback to find that there were quite a few people already in the club. A pair here, a group there and a few people sitting alone on barstools near her. She peered around this darkened place, vaguely recognizing some people whom she thought may know Jink's whereabouts.

****

Her eyes locked on two men and a woman sitting on the other side of the room. When a voice behind her spoke up,

"Hi Gwen, I haven't seen you in awhile. How you been?"

Gwen turned around and saw the bartender smiling while drying a glass and putting it in a rack with other glasses its size.

"Oh! Hi, Barry!"
"Can I get you something to drink?"
"Yes, can I get a Coke?"
"Coke. Anything else? Johnson just came in and he's got the grill on now. We can have a sandwich or a burger done in about... 15 minutes?"
"No, thank you. That's okay. Barry, can I ask you a question?"
"Sure. What do you need to know?"
"I was wondering... did you hear.... do you know when Jink is coming back?"
"Jink! Yeah, I just heard those guys talking about it last night and this morning. They said his flight gets in today about noon. That girl over there works for him. I overheard her say that Jink's coming by here at around 4 and that she had better have his money ready."
"That girl over there with those two guys?"

"Yeah, that's her. She's one of his 'wife-in-laws'!"

"Wife-in-laws! What's that?"

"Yeah, wife-in-law! That's a woman who's like a wife but ain't one legally. She's been with him for a while. She met Jink after he married the girl whose mother owns that fish fry shop up the street by Big Liz's house. Yeah, you might even be considered another one of his wife-in-laws."

"Me? He's married! How could he be married? Who's he married to?"

"Oh, come on now, Gwen, don't pretend as if you don't know?"

Gwen stood silent for a second.

"Barry, I need to talk to them over there. Can I have that Coke now?"

"Sure," Barry said. "Here you go." Barry threw the white towel over his shoulder and went back to the sink to get another glass to dry.

Gwen walked over to the group she was staring at when she first came in. She knew both of the men as being very friendly with Jink. Jink would normally put his arms around them and point to Gwen before they'd walk off and talk about something outside of Gwen's hearing. Once they were done, they'd wave to Gwen on their way out of the bar. But, now they were addressing her personally, which never happened when Jink was around. Their hospitality threw Gwen for a loop for a second. One of the guys raised his arms to hug her and squeeze her tight. The other man and woman just laughed.

"Gwen, Gwen, Gwen! Lemme look at 'cha! Where ya' bin, girl? I ain't seen much of ya since Jink gone."

"I've been fine. Barry tells me that you know when Jink's coming right?"

"Ol' Jink should be arriving any minute. He bin asking 'bout ya an eveythang. We tole' him that we was keepin' an eye out for ya. So, eveythang's good girl."

"Keeping an eye out for me? Why? He knows where to find me." Gwen said with a look of suspicion as she saw the other man and woman laughing.

She looked at the woman carefully. She looked familiar, but she looked like one of the women who'd stop Jink on the street and ask to talk to him privately when they were out on a date. The woman was staring back at Gwen, looking her up and down while chewing gum and blowing big bubbles in Gwen's face.

"Jink likes to know that everything is level when he's not around. That's all that this fool should have said," the other guy standing next to the prostitute said to Gwen. "Don't worry. He knows you're alright. He's got people to keep him abreast of what's going on in the neighborhood and he's had a few people to check up on you every now and then."

"Me? Why does he need to check up on me? He can just call or send me a letter," Gwen said.

"That's just Jink. He don't trust nobody."

Gwen shook her head in amazement. Then she noticed the woman talking with the first man. Leaning over, she whispered something in his ear; then he nodded while giggling.

"Gwen," the first man spoke, "we gat somefin fa ya. It's a new candy we 'bout to sell in the street and in the sto'es, why don't ya try it out and let us know what ya thank?"

"Oh, I don't think so. I better get going. I'm coming back to see Jink later," Gwen said.

"Here ya go. We ain't selfish 'round heyer. Try dis... come on. Stick out ya tongue!"

Gwen was reluctant at first. Looking at them and by the smell of them, she knew it had been at least several days since any of them had seen a shower. But still, she opened her mouth.

The first man laid a thin strip of what looked like a small square about the size of a fingernail. It was translucent but because the bar was somewhat dark, Gwen couldn't tell if it had a green or bluish tint. Either way, the first guy peeled it off of a piece of aluminum foil and dropped it on the tip of Gwen's tongue.

Gwen closed her mouth and immediately felt this clear strip start to dissolve and burn her tongue. She started to walk off when the three people stood in front of her and lead her back to a seat at a stall.

"Girl," the woman said, "you don't be needing to go out there right now. You need to give it a few moments and then you'll be alright."

Gwen was a bit confused by this woman's concern, but as her heart begin to race and her head got very light, Gwen couldn't think properly. She tried to stand up but fell against one of the men. She looked up, and in a vision that multiplied itself into three parts, saw Barry coming toward her. Dark, cloudy figures approached him from the right and the left, but she could barely make out what he was saying to her as he knelt before her.

"I'm alright Barry, I think. I just need some water. Water...please."

She saw the fuzzy image of the bartender stand up and turn

around fast. Two of the people laid her down on a seat as images of Gwen's past came rushing at her in every direction. There were images of people and places she hadn't been before. She saw familiar faces, but she couldn't remember their names immediately. A moment later, they helped her up, and shortly afterward Barry held a glass of water helping her to drink.

Gwen pushed the glass away.

"I gotta go now. My man's coming back and I need to be ready for him."

Gwen stumbled along and was walking out the door when Barry put her handbag on her shoulder and opened her free hand to put the laundry bag in it. He held the door open and the bright light caused Gwen to jump back.

"Gwen, are you going to be alright?"
"Yes, I'm okay. I gotta go now. I'll see you later."

Gwen walked down the block, looking down at the sidewalk to avoid the sun. Gwen started to have a funny feeling. As she reached the corner to turn up the block to head home, the old, broken and cracked sidewalk squares became nicely paved. Gone was the faded, bleached gray cement, but now a newly spread, dark gray pavement. With each step Gwen noticed hand prints and foot prints started to appear in them. Signatures began to write themselves over prints.

She looked up and street signs disappeared. Restaurants and grocery store signs disappeared as well. Couples in dress shirts and ties, long gowns and lace ups became young people wearing sunglasses, t-shirts, swim trunks and sandals. The girls who were beside them wore their hair up and were wearing one-piece bathing suits. Over and behind them, the Hollywood marquis rose in place of the highway signs.

Gwen looked down again and saw paved square tiles displaying the names of Judy Garland, Frank Sinatra, Louis Armstrong and Burt Lancaster. The more she walked, the more she saw the entertainers she loved and recognized in the squares leading to her place. But as she kept walking, she came across an empty square. She stood over it for a second and her signature started to write itself on the pavement. "Gwendolyn Collins." Then her hand prints appeared underneath it.

Gwen's heart began to race. She looked around her and there was a crowd clapping and throwing kisses at her. Gwen smiled and waved at her fans. She looked and didn't see her footprints. She stepped out of her white high-heeled pumps and lifted up her white flowing gown and stepped onto the soft pavement in her sheer stockings. She felt the earth move underneath her foot. She shimmied it into the place to create her footprint.

A man in a tuxedo helped Gwen out of the space. Gwen curtsies to him and looked back at her step. The impression of her footsteps began to disappear. Gwen kicked her shoes off again and immediately tried to replace her footsteps; they disappeared. Next, her hand prints. Frustrated, Gwen jumped on the space and started to dig her feet in, but the ground wouldn't move beneath her. To make matters worse, the pavement began to turn light gray and hard. She dug down deeper, but the pavement wouldn't move. Soon all of the surrounding pavement squares around her begin to turn old and dingy. The names of the celebrities disappeared as did the Hollywood sign in the distance.

Gwen looked around, and the crowds around her that were clapping and calling out her name changed, and people stood leaning against parked cars were pointing and laughing at her. She was embarrassed, that drug had a quick hallucinating effect on her. She turned around and saw the three people who were in Candyman's laughing hysterically behind her. She looked down and saw the torn skin and scuff marks she made trying to make an impression on the dirty sidewalk where she stood. 'Oh shoot,' she said to herself, feeling stupid for taking that drug.

She carefully put her feet back into her sandals, picked up her laundry bag and purse and slowly walked home. Whatever it was that man gave her, the effect was over, but she still had a bit of a headache and sore, bloody feet to show for it.

****

Some hours had passed since Gwen came home. She had taken a shower, folded her clean clothes and put them up. She pulled two sets of clothes out and laid them on her bed. She couldn't decide which one to wear to see Jink.

Sitting on the bed made her think about some of the things she heard this morning and about the LSD she received from those guys there. The drug overdose was one thing. Jink being married and not admitting it and the chances are that he is indeed a pimp was too much news for her to accept. How could he do this to me? Why would he do this? He's smart, good-looking, charming, why would he need to stoop to such things? Gwen was also concerned with the fact that she was now showing a little bit. What am I going to say to him? Congratulations! You're going to be a daddy! But, there were too many things to discuss and breaking the news that he was going to be a father felt like a bad idea. So, Gwen decided on some loose fitting clothes to hide her situation.

She stood in front of the bed and closed her eyes and pointed her finger over each set of clothes.

> Eeeny, meeny, miney, mo.
> Put the baby on the po.
> When he's done,
> Wipe his bum
> And tell his mother what he's done.

With that, Gwen chose the outfit closest to her hand. She took a deep breath after she looked at herself in the mirror. She wondered if he'd prefer the other outfit to the one she was wearing. 'Never mind,' she thought to herself. She walked out of the door and remembered to lock it with the key. She didn't want Terri showing up again if she brought Jink back home tonight.

**** ****

Gwen brushed her feet at the doorstep of Candyman's, while waiting for a couple to exit out. They extended the door to her and she found herself standing in the doorway where she was some 6 hours before. This time, she knew she was finally going to see her man, Jink.

She waved to Barry who came by the end of the counter closest to the door and asked if she was okay. Gwen told him she was fine and that whatever they gave her, she was back to one hundred percent.

In the noisy and crowded club-bar, she asked where Jink was. Barry walked the length of the bar and came back before pointing to a corner diagonal from where they were standing. Gwen stood on the balls of her feet. She smiled as she saw the back of Jink sitting at a booth talking with a woman. She thanked Barry again and made her way through the crowd until she was a few feet away from Jink.

As she approached, the woman who was sitting with Jink motioned with her head to Jink to look in Gwen's direction. Jink turned to Gwen as she came toward him but turned back to the woman and continued his conversation.

Seeing this, Gwen stopped and looked at Jink in surprise. 'What is he thinking? Doesn't he recognize me? Maybe he didn't recognize me?' A flood of thoughts came to her head.

"Hi, Jink! Welcome home, baby!"

Jink continued to talk with the woman without skipping a beat.

"Excuse me. I said, Hello, Jink. Welcome home!'

Jink continued talking in the same volume as he had before but this time, he put his hand behind him and waved Gwen off. Gwen stood there in silence. A feeling of panic, embarrassment and fear came over her.

"So, you're just going to sit there and ignore me like you don't even know me, huh?"

Jink touched the woman's hand as if to say, give me a moment. Then Jink turned around to face Gwen.

"Yes. What do you want? Can't you see I'm busy?"
"Jink, why are you talking to me this way. What happened to you?"
"No, the question is, what happened to you. I left you specific orders on how to behave when I'm gone and I get reports that

you're doing this and you're doing that. I hear that you're asking questions about me and my private life, getting up in my business with people you don't even know. And, you have the nerve to ask me, if there's anything wrong with me."

Gwen looked shocked at such a rebuke.

"Jink, wait, I don't know what you heard, but it ain't like that. I don't know what you're talking about."

"You don't know what I'm talking about? You don't know what I'm talking about? That sounds so funny. Listen, I'm going to tell you something. Ain't nothing going down in this town without me knowing it or allowing it. You hear me? I even know where all the roaches live and what they had for dinner."

"I have no idea what you're talking about."

"Okay. What's this I hear that you're living with a woman? You turned dike now? Everybody's been telling me that you've shacked up with that dike. You're going to tell me that you're not living with a dike? You're not sleeping with her?"

"No, Jink. I don't know anything about her personal life. She lived with me for two weeks because she was homeless. I took her in because she was sleeping outside in the rain. That's it, Jink. No, I haven't slept with her."

"You think I'm a fool, huh?" Jink went into his pocket and pulled out a few bills and threw it on the table. He looked back at the woman who was his guest and said, "Babe, let's pick this up later. I need you to be there when he gets out of his conference and take care of his every need. I'll call you about two o'clock to check up on you."

"Jink," Gwen said, "What's that all about? Are you a pimp? Is she a prostitute? Jink, are you married?"

"You ask a lot of questions. I'm a businessman. I make money. She works for me. That's all you need to know. Don't try to change the conversation. Take me to your apartment."

"You want to come to my apartment? Okay."

Both Gwen and Jink walked out of the door and walked roughly a block without saying a word to each other when Jink looked at Gwen,

"On second thought, I don't want to go to your apartment. I would be disgusted at the filth I'd see. You know, you surprise me. I'm really disappointed in you. I thought I knew you better but you're just like the rest of them."

"The rest of who? I'm trying to figure out why are you so mad at me? What did I do wrong?"

"You still playing little Miss Innocent. Okay, we're gonna play a little game. It's called the Game of Truth. You ask me a question, I tell you the truth. I ask you a question, you tell me the truth. Got it?"

"Okay. You never answered my questions. Are you a pimp? Was that one of your prostitutes? And...oh, are you married?"

"The answers to all of those questions..." Jink said, parting his full three-quarter length, white Italian suit, "...is yes."

Gwen stood back and put her hand over her mouth.

"Take your hand away from your mouth and stop looking so surprised. How do you think I'm able to afford all of the stuff I got and what I got you? It ain't by working some jive job for $1.50/ hr. You want me to work at some burger joint flipping burgers while Nixon is sitting on all that money and don't want to give people a good salary to take care of themselves? I'm taking care of me. I'm taking care of my girls. And, as for you, had you been faithful to me, this is what you would have gotten."

Jink reached into his jacket's side pocket and pulled out a long box. He opened it and four different diamond rings were perched inside this felt-lined body.

"I was going to give this to you, but now, I'm going to give it to my new number one lady in Germany."

"I'm sorry, Jink, if you feel like I betrayed you, but I didn't. I didn't do anything wrong."

"Okay, it's my turn. I hear you lost the job at the phone company. Where have you been getting the money to survive and to keep a roof over your head?"

"A friend just got me a job at the Holiday Inn. I start next week cleaning rooms."

"Oh, so you're going to tell me that you've never been in need of money. You been doing drugs?"

"No!"

"No! Oh, really. So, you mean to tell me that you weren't smoking a blunt or two with Delores?"

"You know Miss Delores?'

"Do I know Miss Delores? Everybody knows Delores. I told you already. Ain't nothing going down in the street without me knowing it. I'll tell you what, that's one lie I caught you in, maybe two if you count that dike as another. But, I'm going to take you to meet someone. She'll tell me everything I need to know."

"Who's this?"

"We're going to see my friend, Big Liz!"

"Who is Biz Liz?"

******

Big Liz, was a mysterious woman who was known to exist by almost everyone who traveled through downtown Charleston. Not many people knew exactly what she looked like and even fewer people knew where she lived. All they knew was that she was available for whatever "pharmaceutical products" she offered, and whatever services to those who participated in clandestine soirees needed.

Big Liz lived at the end of Court Street right next to a woman who owned a small fish fry restaurant. Gwen would find out that Liz's house was literally on the corner of that popular fish fry joint. On their way, Gwen asked Jink why'd they call this woman "Big Liz?" Jink, after about a minute of silence trying to decide whether or not to answer her, looked straight ahead and told her that Liz was big and tall and had wide hips.

"Very hippy, I guess? I don't remember why we call her that but she's got a big butt. Maybe that's why."

They made their way up the dark street. Turned a corner, walked a few more blocks all the way down an increasingly darker street called, "Frye's Alley." Jink, about a step ahead of Gwen, turned to her and said:

"Just follow me and whatever you do, don't ask any questions."

They walked through a yard and up some narrow side steps that led to a kitchen door. Gwen walked very slowly and carefully up the stairs until she looked up and noticed Jink staring down at her. Jink knocked on the door. The door opened and there stood Big Liz. She barely parted her lips and grumbled something to Jink that sounded like "Welcome Back," but Gwen couldn't be too certain. Then Big Liz looked at Gwen who stood on the steps just below Jink.

Big Liz was intimidating to look at, at least that was Gwen's first impression. If Gwen had to guess, she'd probably say that Big Liz was around 5'11" and weighed about three hundred and twenty pounds. She had beautiful "good" hair and caramel colored skin.

One thing that jumped out at Gwen was Big Liz' appearance...she wore big pearls. The pearls draped her low-cut blouse. She wasn't big on top but when Gwen sized her up, she sort of looked look like a pear. Still, Big Liz refused to greet her.

Big Liz turned around and walked in. Jink opened the screen door and walked in. He made sure to give Gwen that reminder look to be quiet and ask no questions no matter what she saw. When Gwen walked through the door, she indeed found herself in the kitchen.

The kitchen was somewhat dark. The walls, the table, and the chairs, were also dark and drabby. Two people who sat at the table had several rows of a white powder substance in front of them. They looked at Gwen before one of them leaned down and continued sniffing this white powder that was already on his face.

Gwen continued walking straight ahead until she saw an opening there in the middle of the room. There was Big Liz and Jink talking in a low voice. Gwen looked around and saw various people in different stages of consciousness. Some were on an old beat up couch; others were stooped down against the wall. There were some prostitutes that Gwen had recognized from the streets as well that were staring at her from across the room.

Gwen walked over to Jink who had stopped talking to Liz and was waiting for her to come over.

"Now, I'm going to ask you one more time," Jink said to Gwen, *"and don't lie to me."*

Then Jink turned to Liz and asked her several questions about Gwen pertaining to drug use, prostitution, Terri and Delores. Each time Gwen denied the obvious. And each time, Liz looked at

Jink and told him that Gwen was lying.

"Okay. I heard enough. *I know what you were doing because I also heard the same thing from my right-hand man...you know, the boyfriend of one of your friends."*

Gwen looked petrified.

"Yeah, that one. I know all about it. You're just like the rest of them."
"No, I'm not!" Gwen pleaded, "No, I'm not!"

Gwen stood there and cried as Jink walked past her and into the kitchen. Gwen stood there crying for several minutes until she realized that Jink hadn't returned for her. She looked up and Liz was standing near the entrance of kitchen talking with one of her girls. Liz stopped her conversation and looked to a red-eyed, Gwen,

"He left a few minutes ago. I think you'd better leave before you get yourself into any more trouble."

Gwen walked past Liz without uttering a response. She walked through the kitchen and made her way to the outside steps. Gwen stood staring in the dark, hoping to catch a glimpse of a 5'8" man in a three-piece suit and a tilted fedora hat. There were not many who dressed like Jink, but Gwen could pick him out in a crowd.

******

She looked around and saw a light in a room in a building across the street. She looked up and down the street and it didn't appear as if Jink had taken that route. She looked again at a light shining from the room upstairs. This time, she saw the silhouette of a man in a suit walking around and other shadows moving in and out. It was enough for Gwen to investigate. She knew she couldn't sleep if she didn't try to make up with Jink.

She walked up three flights of stairs and when she got to the top floor, she knocked very lightly. She didn't want to disturb a loud conversation that was going on inside. She knocked again, this time just a little bit harder. The door unlatched from the lock and slowly opened.

"Hello?" Gwen said softly. "Hello...is anyone there?" Still no answer although she could still hear talking just beyond the door.

Gwen pushed the door open little by little and once she was able to get a view of the room with the light on, she pushed the door a little wider. This time, she saw the man with a white fedora hat tilted to the side. He was kneeling down in front of someone with two women standing on opposite sides of him looking down at the person in front of him.

Gwen walked in, recognizing Jink and putting down her emotions. She fought through the fear of being caught and made peace within herself, that she'd come clean with him and would beg for his forgiveness if that's what it took to make things right.

As Gwen walked to the group in front of her, one of the women turned to look at her and smiled. She wore a silver wig and a gleeful smile. But upon further inspection, the woman had bristles of hair that started to grow back over her lips and a big Adam's apple that went in when this deep voice said,

"Oh, hi. Are you looking for someone?"

Another person on the other side of Jink had on very thick eyeliner and a pink blush that almost glimmered off of their shiny silver wig. Gwen realized that these women were really men. Both men wore dresses all the way down to their calf. The man on the left wore an off-white sandal that draped around his ankle. The man on the right wore a black pump that had his bunions bulging out on the sides as if the shoes had been worn well past its life cycle.

Gwen was silent for a moment as she quickly nodded but took a step to see what Jink was doing. She walked around and stooped down as she came to his right side, putting her hands on his shoulder. Jink was face to face with a transvestite who was wheelchair bound. The man's arms rested firmly on the armrests.

The three seconds or so felt like three hours in time. Jink turned to see who was touching him and saw a frightened Gwen staring at him. Jink stood up and without saying anything to anyone, including the numerous transvestites that were all around the room, he walked out of the apartment.

Gwen followed suit, running down the same stairs that she had cautiously climbed. She caught Jink just as he made it down to the bottom of the stairs.

    "Jink...Jink... wait... wait...I wanna talk to you. Jink! Jink, wait!" Gwen said panting as she reached out to him.
    "Don't ask me nothing, you hear?"
    "Jink, Jink... I'm sorry. I just want to talk to you for a minute." Gwen said as she clutched his arm. "Jink, why didn't you tell me? Don't you think I would have wanted to know?"
    "Know what? You ask too many questions. First, you lie to me and you do drugs and you steal and I have to find out, you been hoeing around."
    "But, Jink..."

"But, Jink, nothing. You got nothing to say to me."

"Jink, I love you. Can't you see that? What about all the time we spent together? And, what about the plans we made to get married and buy a house and settle down?"

Jink stopped walking and turned to Gwen,

"That wasn't my plan, that was yours. I never told you I wanted that."

"But, Jink, what about us? What was that about upstairs?"

"You need to mind your business. Okay. I'm gonna come clean with you so you can rest. Yes, I'm married. Yes, I'm a pimp. Yes, I do drugs and yes, about upstairs... I'm into that too." Jink looked at Gwen whose eyes and mouth were wide open. "Close your mouth and stop acting so surprised. You weren't born yesterday."

Jink turned from Gwen buttoned his top button and began to walk briskly down the long dark street. Gwen quickly followed but saying nothing for fear that she might learn something else she was not ready to know.

As they approached the lighted area around Court Street, Gwen tugged on Jink's jacket,

"Jink, what am I going to do? I have nowhere else to go."

Jink stopped and paused for a moment. He gazed into the deep reaches of the midnight sky, as he lowered his head, he saw the street names plastered at the intersection,

"It seems to me you got four directions you could go."

With that, Jink shrugged his jacket away from Gwen's grip and walked into a bar. Gwen stood there for a second and started to cry before she began walking in the direction of her apartment.

sixteen

All through the course of the night ever since she left Jink, his words haunted her. "You think you're in control of your life, huh? I'm in control. I am. What's my name? If it weren't for me, I wouldn't know where you'd be. I run this show. ME! Everything you got is because of me. I'm your daddy!"

'Who does he think he is? I buy my own clothes. In fact, I buy his. I found my own job and I make my own money. Not him!' Gwen fought the sound of his words with her own thoughts as she stared up at the ceiling.

Gwen walked around her apartment. She looked at her clothes, her high heels and a few books and magazines. Lifting up a few issues of Vogue and Cosmopolitan and resting them back down on her nightstand. She even looked at the bedspread. All of it. All of it, Gwen paid for it herself.

She closed her eyes and wondered how did she make a mistake getting mixed up with a guy like Jink. 'Why doesn't he respect me? Who does he think he is? I'm my own woman. Can't nobody

talk to me like that!' Gwen went back to bed satisfied.
Gwen woke up to the sound of a knock at her door. When she opened the door, she saw two hands touching each other at the top of their fingertips and covering the eyes of the woman behind them.

The woman parted her hands and Gwen recognized the smiling face as Vicky.

   "Hi, Gwen! How ya' doing?"

Hugging Gwen, Vicky continued,

   "I haven't seen you around in a while!"
   "Vicky, Oh my god! It's so good to see you! Come in!"

Gwen made coffee for them and after some small chatter, Gwen went on to describe the details of her confrontation with Jink. Gwen would see Vicky close her eyes and shake her head as she told her specifics. Oftentimes she'd pick up Vicky murmuring her displeasure.

   "Girl, let's go for a walk. I think you need some fresh air. Come with me to the post office. I've got to mail these bills off so I won't get a late fee."

Gwen and Vicky head out to the post office.

   "Gwen, the problem with men is that they think when we give them some, they own us. NO! No man owns me. I give it to him because I want to."

Vicky looked at Gwen; her attention was temporarily distracted by the women in Delores's apartment. Gwen stooped down to adjust the strap on her three-inch heels.

"What we need Gwen, is to fast!"

"Fast?" Gwen stood up as if she was hearing a foreign language. "Fast, like in what... not eating? How's starving to death make my man respect me?"

"Uhhhh, Gwen, I'm not talking about food, I'm talking about taking a break from men. You gotta find yourself. You gotta claim your independence from him. That's the only way he's gonna respect you. Look, ain't no man gonna respect you when you running under him like he's some god. And, Jink ain't no god. He's a little runt."

Gwen kept her silence as she looked at Vicky from the corner of her eyes.

"You need to leave that zero. He's a big, fat, zero!"

Gwen put her hand up,

"He's still my man no matter what right now... for the time being at least, so cut him a little slack...just for me?"

Vicky rolled her eyes.

"You can do so much better than him unless you're telling me that you like drama."

"Vicky, please just drop it. I don't wanna talk about Jink no more. I have other things on my mind. I'm about to lose my job at the phone company. I've got rent coming up, I need grocery money and... and, I'm just under a lot of stress now."

"You can always find another job. The phone company is not the only game in town."

"Vicky, I need money. I need a lot of money. You can't comprehend what I'm going through."

"Yes, I can. I've lost jobs, I found jobs. I gave up boyfriends and I found others. I know what you're going through."

"I think I'm pregnant."

"I- WHAT! Pregnant? What do you mean? How do you know? Who....?"

"I haven't had my period in a couple of months."

"Well, how..."

Gwen adjusted her bag and stared at the cracks on the pavement as she continued to walk without looking at Vicky.

"I think it's with this other guy that I met a few months ago. I met him at this dance and he told me he went to the Job Corps in his state. Then one thing led to another and we took a walk and I found myself in this wooded area behind a school. I don't remember what happened after that."

"Why did it take so long for you to know?"

"Because of my metabolism, my periods would come at different times of the month. I totally forgot about it and I've been thinking that I'm just bloated."

"Well, what are you going to do?"

"I don't know. I feel like my world's falling apart... my job, my man, my apartment, I can't go back to Kentucky. I've got no one to help me.

"I'm here for you."

"I know, but I need money. I need a lot of money. And, if I'm pregnant, I'm gonna need even more money."

"Can you get money from Jink?"

"Jink? Jink can't know about this. I've got to deal with this on my own. I don't know how I'm gonna get this money."

Vicky took a deep breath,

"C'mon, let's get some pizza after I mail off these letters, okay?"

They walked a few blocks and as they opened the door to the building where the post office was located, Gwen turned to a group of people passing by a counter in the lobby on the right-hand side.

The people in front of the counter were dropping coins in a dish, each saying something to the blind man who was sitting in the corner at the end of the counter. All of the customers seemed to know the gentleman and addressed him by his first name. And he seemed to recognize them by their voice and remembered what they usually came for.

As Gwen waited in the lobby for Vicky to return, she noticed the old, blind man occasionally walk to the opposite end of the counter. He'd stoop down and pick up a beige canvas bag, open it and squeeze the bills that he took from the counter and shove them into the bag before pulling the drawstring. Then he'd put the bag back in the very spot he picked it up from.

Gwen's mind started racing. Behind the chair where he sat was a door to a storeroom. Every now and then he would go inside and then come back out. Gwen turned around and saw that Vicky was next in line.

Vicky came out of the double glass doors with a look of relief on her face, when she noticed Gwen placed her pointer finger against her lips and motioned for her to come over quickly and quietly. Vicky's expression turned to concern because she knew whatever it was Gwen was scheming, it might not be good.

"Okay," Gwen said as she lowered her voice, "here's the plan!"
"Plan! What are you talking about?"
"Okay, you're-"
"Me!"

"You're going to ask the blind man for something while I get the money," Gwen said that as she turned around to see if anyone was behind her.

"What money? What are you talking about?"

"Shhhh! Just do as I say. Wait until after these people leave then go up to him and ask him for a bottle of ginger ale."

"Ginger ale? I don't even like ginger ale."

"Vicky, I need you to do this for me." Gwen stood up straight. "I know I'm pregnant and I don't have any money for when the hospital bills come."

Vicky looked for a question to ask in response, then tried to think of a reason to say, no.

"Okay, but don't blame me if we get caught."
"I won't," Gwen said, beaming.

They waited about fifteen minutes, as there was a constant stream of people walking through the foyer to go to the post office. Finally, after a while the bustle died down. Gwen nudged Vicky,

"Here," giving Vicky a hand full of nickels. "If it looks like he hears me drop these on the counter in front of him."

As Vicky walked over to the corner where the blind man sat, Gwen's heart started to race. It was the same kind of nervousness she had when she'd sneak out of the house after everyone went to bed and she'd run through the graveyard to get to the jazz club in Madisonville.

When Gwen saw the old man open the door and walk inside, she quickly looked around and walked briskly to the opposite side of the counter. She leaned over to the counter and as she felt the top of the bag with her fingertips, she noticed it was just beyond her grasp to pick it up. She looked down the aisle to see the old man coming from out of the room.

Although he was saying something to Vicky, he was facing in Gwen's direction. He held the can of soda in his hand but he stood still, almost as if he could see Gwen laying on top of the counter and reaching for his money-bag.

"Sir," Vicky said, "I'm over here. Can I pay you for the drink?"

The old man said nothing but laid the can down on the counter in front of Vicky. He took one step in the direction towards Gwen, when Vicky grabbed his hand and dropped all of the coins Gwen gave her in his hand and on the counter.

As the sound of the coins hitting the counter started to resonate, Gwen pushed herself more over the countertop until she could reach further down to hoist up the bag. She slowly shifted her weight until she felt herself slipping off the counter to then tiptoe out the door.

Vicky looked around to see if people in line had noticed, but when she saw Gwen walking out the door, she immediately ran to catch up with her, leaving the can of soda behind. As she reached the door, she turned around one last time and noticed the blind man on the opposite side of the counter stooping down. She ran to catch up with Gwen.

Gwen and Vicky walked down the street looking at each other and giggling. They felt the anxiety subside the further they were from the post office, but feeling guilty because of his disability.

"I don't feel like pizza. Wanna get something to drink?" Gwen said as she saw a Coca-Cola sign next to the store's marquis.

"Yeah, I'm thirsty," Vicky said as she reached into her back pocket for a dollar bill.

They stood in line to pay for their soda pops when Gwen nudged Vicky to turn around.

"Do you think we should give it back?"
"If we go back there," Vicky said, "we could get caught."

Gwen tapped the bottle cap with her finger,

"I feel bad. Maybe he doesn't have food at home? Maybe he has a family?"
"We need the money, too. People will always give him money." Vicky responded.
"I know," Gwen said softly. "I know."

They walked a few blocks in silence, each sipping a small amount of pop and wondering if what they did was right and thinking of a reason to pacify their consciences. When they turned the corner onto Capitol Street, Gwen looked at Vicky and said,

"We still need more money. I just need a little more to pay the rest of my bills. What we have won't even be enough to pay some of my phone bill."

Vicky stopped and looked at Gwen,

"How we gonna get more? Do you know anybody else we can rob?"

Gwen shook her head and thought to herself, 'This is not how I want to make it. I can't keep robbing people to eat.'
Vicky was about to say something when a long black car slowly

pulled up beside them. An older man, perhaps a man in his mid-70's, leaned over to look through the passenger side. He stopped the car and manually rolled down the window.

"Excuse me! Excuse me, young ladies!"

Gwen and Vicky walked over to the car and leaned down, both thinking that he needed directions.

"I'm sorry to bother you but would one of you like to sit down and talk with me for a few minutes? I'd be more than happy to pay you for your time."

Both of the women shrugged their shoulders, but Vicky turned to Gwen and raised her eyebrows. Then she turned to the elderly, gentleman,

"Excuse me, sir. Can we both come? I don't wanna leave my friend alone."

The gentleman was silent for a moment,

"Sure, sure! I wasn't expecting to see two beautiful women today, but sure!"

He reached behind the passenger's side and pulled up the lock. He pulled on the door lever to open it. Vicky quickly reached for the passenger's side and Gwen walked slowly to the back door. After they were in, the elderly man looked around and said openly,

"Well, young ladies, is there anywhere we can go to talk privately?"

Gwen leaned forward,

"Sir, where do you wanna go?"
"Oh, I don't know...maybe somewhere where it's less traffic. It could be somewhere close."

Vicky looked and Gwen, and then looked at the gentleman,

"Let's go by that area near the expressway. Hardly anybody walks by there. Only cars speeding to get onto the expressway drive by. So, no one can really see us."

The gentleman drove in the direction of those pointing fingers and turned off the car.

"Okay, now. Uhhh... I wanna ask you something and I hope that I don't offend you."

Gwen looked at Vicky and they both shrugged their shoulders again.

"I want to know if you ladies are working ladies?"

Gwen looked at Vicky and they wondered what to answer. Vicky slowly turned to him and said,

"We...we... make friends with people, if that's what you mean?"

The gentleman stared at her for a second and then looked at Gwen,

"Friends?"
"Yeah, friends," Gwen said, unconvincingly.
"Well, uhmm, I'd like to be friends with you. Well, maybe just one of you." He looked at Vicky, "How much do I have to pay to

have a friend?"

Vicky looked at Gwen, but Gwen was puzzled to silence. Vicky swallowed a little bit of saliva,

"Twenty-five dollars."
"Oh, uhmm, I wasn't exactly thinking it would be that much. Could we be friends for maybe fifteen?" he said, as he tilted his head.

Gwen leaned in.

"We can be friends for twenty."
"Twenty!" he said, with a sigh. *"Okay."* He looked at Vicky. Then looked at Gwen. Turning to Vicky, *"Excuse me, I hope you won't be offended, but could I talk with her?"*

Vicky smiled and looked at Gwen.

"No, sir. That's all right. She's my friend. I'll sit here and keep a lookout, okay?"

The gentleman tapped Vicky on her leg,

"I really appreciate it. I didn't know how you'd take it."
"I'm a big girl," Vicky said with a smile.

He walked out of the car and opened the rear door to the back seat and sat down next to Gwen. He started to perspire. Gwen looked at him,

"Sir, it's alright. There's nothing to be scared of. I'm your friend. I won't hurt you and I'm not here to judge you, either."
"Thank you. I needed to hear that." He took Gwen's left hand and started to caress it softly. *"When I saw you, you looked just like my wife when we first met."*

He looked around and saw Vicky watching from the front seat.
"Should I pay now?"

Vicky was startled,

"Oh, yeah, you can if you want."

The gentleman reached into his back pocket and pulled out a large, leather wallet. It was stuffed with papers and a few old, faded pictures. He withdrew a twenty-dollar bill and handed it over to Vicky. As he was about to put it back in his pocket, he opened his billfold up wide and showed them a picture of him and his wife on their wedding day.

"She's beautiful," Gwen said, looking at the face and the dress.
"She passed away about twelve years ago. Today would have been our fifty-third wedding anniversary. So...so... I just...I've been alone for a long, long time now and I miss her a lot. Our children are all grown up and they hardly ever call. I haven't seen my grand-babies in... I don't know when, to be honest with you. So, I just wanted to...."

Just at that moment, tears fell from his eyes. Gwen held his hand and kissed the top of it. Slowly, she rested his hand on her lap. The gentleman slowly moved his hand around her knee. He turned, adjusting himself on the seat as to face to face to Gwen.

Gwen squirmed with every pinch. She looked away because it felt strange to let someone else touch her now that Jink was back in town. Gwen felt his pulse increase and she fought to stay still.

Gwen gripped his arm and closed her eyes. 'It would only be a few minutes,' she thought, as she pictured herself running down the street from her grandmother Cecil's house, being chased by her brother Michael. 'Happy thoughts,' is what she tried to force herself to think of. It would be her best escape.

Suddenly he stopped.

"Thank you," the elderly man said between breaths. "I know that I'll probably never see you again, but you have no idea what this means to me. I want you to know that I never cheated on my wife before. All of those years we were together, I was..."
"Sir," Gwen said, "you don't have to apologize. I understand."

Gwen leaned up and fixed her bra and adjusted her panty.

"Okay," he said. "I need to be going now. Can I drop you off where we met? Do you want me to drop you off someplace else?"

Vicky looked at Gwen,

"It's okay. We can walk back from here."
"Are you sure, it's no trouble for me."
"We'll be alright," Gwen said.

Both Gwen and Vicky came out of the car at the same time, while the elderly gentleman remained in the back seat for a few moments. As they walked away, they turned back to see him standing by the driver's side looking at them. They made eye contact, then the gentleman went into his car and slowly drove on the expressway.

Gwen and Vicky silently they walked back to Gwen's apartment. They sat on the bed and counted up all of the money. Vicky pushed half of the pile next to Gwen, then placed a twenty-dollar bill on top of it.

"Why'd you do that?" Gwen said.

"This is from the old man. You earned it. I didn't."

"But, we're in this together."

"I know, but you were like a pastor to him."

17

"Everybody's goin' to a BBF, and taking their appetite.

Everybody's goin' to a BBF at the whirling satellite.

You can eat 'em there, or take 'em home,

And entertaining can be fun.

Let BBF be your party chef.

Serve a banquet on a bun!"

Charleston, despite the visible underside of the downtown area, was, for the most part, a family-friendly city.

This industrial and commercial center of the nineteenth century gradually gave way to a modern metropolis with roadways, ushering in families and businesses from all over the United States. Soon, geographical locations and communities, defined by wealth and which direction you drove to from downtown, determined who you were and what possibilities were afforded to you.

Not to be left out, but the city council did create the North Charleston Recreation Center and the Donnally Street Community Center. It was at the Donnally Street Center in particular where some of the area's and country's best basketball hopefuls would hone their craft. Players and fans from all over the metropolitan and the surrounding suburban areas would congregate and discuss prospects with Universities and NBA scouts.

After a day of basketball or swimming meets, Charleston's local restaurants served as a favorite post-destination for hungry athletes. One of the most well known spots in Charleston is still remembered fondly today. The resting-place of choice was also the home of the best-tasting hamburgers around...Burger Boy Food-O-Rama or simply, "BBF!"

Every weekend, one could see the family car pull up and drop off their teenage kids. This was especially true and a ritual for one of Charleston's favorite sons, West Womack. It was not uncommon to hear a young West thank his mom for dropping him off at BBF after basketball practice.

He was a star basketball player at his high school as well as playing a key role in the next generation of singers in his family from the famous Womack family singers.

But when it came down to getting something to eat after playing in the Washington Manor area, nothing compared to his time at the Burger Boy Food-O-Rama. Nothing. It was a place where he could meet with his friends and listen to all of the Top 40 hits that played on the restaurant's jukebox.

At the time, Burger Boy Food-O-Rama was the only fast food restaurant that had an eat-in dining room. Competitors, McDonald's and Burger Chef only had drive-thru stations with a few token benches out front. But, BBF had them beat with a full dining experience and social atmosphere that was way ahead of its time for the kind of restaurant it was.

Just a few short blocks away, people stood in line at small, private restaurants to order fish and chips. The fish of choice: whiting. Pacific Witting, to be more specific. And boy, do Charlestonians love their deep-fried whiting, breaded in cornmeal especially after a night of partying.

Although Charleston had its share of visible and institutional issues regarding segregation, downtown Charleston was at times a place where different activities encouraged racial integration. Among them was the music scene. Charleston was known to have some of the best jazz clubs in the south. Local and major recording artists would stop in Charleston as one of the "Chitlin' Circuit" stops. You also had R&B and soul singers who would pass through as well. All of this was an attraction for teenagers who lived in the suburbs or areas outside of the downtown Charleston area.

Of course, as in every area and in every town where two or more different racial or cultural communities coexist, you had (and have) miscegenation. And Charleston was no different. At any given time, you'd see white Charlestonians drive around with black Charlestonians and vice versa. What was the intrigue? The older generation from all sides would ask this question, forgetting that they themselves experienced the same thing.

It was not unusual for Gwen to see the irony of discrimination played out Monday through Friday from 9 am to 5 pm, but to see it go topsy-turvy outside of business hours and on the weekends was interesting.

****

Gwen sat on the steps outside of her apartment thinking about Jink, when she noticed a transaction from her view from the steps: a man with whom she used to work with at the phone company. A distinguished white executive, just stopped in front of her building in his Porsche. She recognized the car because he was the only one driving that model and color in town.

Gwen stood up and took a few steps down just to make certain that he was one of the executives she knew of. He looked different in his sky blue sailing shirt and dark glasses, but she knew his hairstyle anywhere and she saw the big ring on his right hand.

The man leaned over and was speaking with someone. At first, Gwen thought he might have been lost and looking for someplace else. But then a female walked up to his car, spoke a few words, then got in. From a distance, the woman looked familiar. But, she couldn't remember from where. After the woman had sat down in the passenger seat, Gwen recognized her as one of the transvestites from that building across from Big Liz' house. The car drove off slowly.

Gwen was thirsty and was tired of drinking water. She tapped her pocket and knew she had enough change for the soda machine that was in front of her building. She made it to the vending machine when a voice behind her yelled,

"Hey! Wanna get high?"

Gwen turned around and saw a tall blonde man in a convertible smiling at her. She held the can of soda in her hand but thought about the pleasure of smoking a joint, which was more appealing right about now. Pepsi or weed? Weed or Pepsi? She ultimately thought of getting high with the cute guy who seemed like a gentleman.

Gwen got in the car and the guy offered to just drive around. Gwen thought of going to a field across from Candyman's but he only wanted to just drive around the block and smoke a joint.

"So... you wanna date?" Gwen said, unsure of his motive.
"Nah, let's just talk and get high. I don't feel like doing anything else," he said.

It was already late in the afternoon and getting darker, so just one joint wouldn't hurt. Besides, she's still in the neighborhood. As he drove, he'd inhale and pass the joint to Gwen.

"So, what's a nice girl like you doing in an area like this?"
"Nothing," Gwen said, "just going out for a walk. I was just getting something to drink."
"It ain't safe being in this neighborhood. You gotta be careful. You don't know who's a friend or not."
"I'm careful. Besides, I've been in this neighborhood for a while now."

The guy began to circle the neighborhood, but the next right turn would have brought them full circle. He didn't take it. Instead, he took and left and followed a winding road that led up a hill. Gwen knew the area and recognized that they were headed in the direction of the cemetery. The car drove, maybe half a mile and stopped several hundred feet onto the cemetery grounds.

"Wait, just a minute. I'm having an engine problem." He tried turning the engine a couple of times, but the engine wouldn't turn over. He opened his door and lifted up the hood. "Excuse me...oh, I didn't get your name?"
"It's Lynn," Gwen said.

"Lynn, do me a favor and turn on the ignition."

Gwen moved over to the driver's seat and turned on the ignition. Nothing. She attempted a couple of more times and still the engine didn't turn over. Finally, the guy dropped the hood and stood by the door,

"Lynne, let's walk back. I know a mechanic and he'll be by tomorrow to tow it."

They walked a few yards when Gwen started to rub her arms to keep warm. The guy, a step behind her, said,

"Lynn, I've got a got a jacket. You can wear it."
"You're such a gentleman! Thank you!"
"Don't wait up for me. I'll be right back," the guy said as Gwen heard his footsteps backtrack in the car's direction.

Gwen must have walked twenty feet when she felt a thump in the back of the head. She fell forward. As she hit the ground, she worried about the impact of her fall on her pregnancy. She turned over to her side when she felt a hard item hit her again in her head. This time, she turned toward him and raised her arms to protect her head while trying to grab the object.

The guy swung several times, beating Gwen's arms as she screamed. When he wasn't able to hit her from where he was, he stepped on her stomach and leaned over to hit her in the forehead.

"Give me your money and I'll stop," he screamed.
"I don't have any money," Gwen cried out.
"Give. Me. Your. Money!" he said angrily, as he continued to stand on her stomach swinging.

Gwen, as hard as it was, wiggled his foot away from the center of her stomach, while clutching on to the tire wrench. He kept screaming at her about the money and she repeated her answer. She realized that she didn't have the strength to keep fighting him off. So, she waited for that moment when he'd pulled back to swing, Gwen reached into her bosom and grabbed a bundle of bills. All eighty-five dollars of it, and threw it in behind him.

The bundle was squashed up, but mostly soaked with the blood that poured from Gwen's head. The money flew in all different directions. Gwen took the opportunity to get up and run down the hill screaming, "HELP! HELP ME! HELP ME! HE'S TRYING TO KILL ME! SOMEBODY, PLEASE HELP ME!"

This went on for several minutes as Gwen made it down the half-mile winding road that led to a residential street. Gwen looked back to see the guy just coming around the bend, just about five hundred feet away from her.

The moment she stopped running, the blood that made a trail from her path now poured down her face. Thinking of nothing else, Gwen screamed again, "SOMEBODY HELP ME! PLEASE, SOMEBODY, HELP ME... HE'S TRYING TO KILL ME!"

Just at that moment, a dark grey pickup truck turned the corner a block away. He was heading in Gwen's direction. Seeing the truck from afar, Gwen ran in front of the pickup truck forcing it to stop. A middle-aged white couple stopped and looked out their window at this screaming, bloody, scared black woman. They were in shock, and they didn't know what to do. The wife tugged on the arm of her husband, he looked at his wife, and then he looked back at Gwen.

Gwen raced to his side of the door and said,

"Please help me. He's trying to kill me!" Pointing over her shoulder.

She pointed at the guy who was now close enough to the couple to be identified. The husband looked behind him in the direction of truck bed and yelled excitedly,

"Get in the back of the truck. Quick!"

The couple sped off leaving the sound of burning rubber vibrating through the neighborhood. They looked back to get a better look at the guy holding a handful of money and a bloody wrench. They witnessed the guy turning around and running back up the hill.

The couple drove a few blocks before the wife opened the window in the cab, and looked out over the truck bed and said,

"Can we take you to the hospital?"
"No...no, please don't. How will I explain what happened? The police will be called and they won't believe me. Can you drop me off on Court Street? My boyfriend lives there," Gwen said as she was squeezing the opening of the gash on top of her head.

She could still feel the blood seeping out but not as much as before. Gwen used the wig that she was wearing to act as a tourniquet of sorts to help stop the heavy flow.

The couple looked at each other when they heard Gwen say, "Court Street." The wife closed the back window and within five minutes, Gwen was standing on Court Street. She held her head to say goodbye to the good samaritan's, but they sped off down the street and disappeared from her view.

****

Gwen had just visited Big Liz' house just a couple of nights before, but she would never forget how to find it. She had hoped that Big Liz would know where Jink was at this time. Gwen knocked on Big Liz' kitchen door. Liz opened the door, saw Gwen and raised her eyelids. Without saying a word, she quickly turned away leaving Gwen standing outside. She briskly walked to the living room and got Jink.

"What were you doing out there by yourself?" Jink screamed at Gwen.
"I...I..."

Gwen couldn't finish her thought or sentence as she was too emotionally distraught.

"I, nothing. I'm asking you again, what were you doing out there and who was this man? Was he a police offer? Was he a trick? Who was he?"

Still, Gwen couldn't answer him. Instead of showing sympathy, Gwen felt that Jink was somehow blaming her for what happened to her.

The tongue-lashing went on unanswered for several minutes. Gwen felt weak and leaned against the wall to hold herself up. Jink, noticed there was something wrong with Gwen and he caught her as she fainted. Gwen woke up a short time later in a hospital bed with an IV in her arm. A nurse was placing a thermometer under her tongue when she opened her eyes.

"Miss Collins, please go back to sleep, you need your rest. The doctor stitched you up. You had a pretty bad fall there and you also have a lot of bruising on your arm. It looks like you were either attacked or in a fight. Do you want to tell us what happened? We didn't quite get the whole story from your boyfriend," the woman said in a very soft and careful tone. She purposely looked away to keep from making eye contact with Gwen. "Let us help you. That's what we're here for," the nurse said as she applied a new bandage to Gwen's head.

"You also lost a lot of blood."

Gwen gave no response, but turned her head to the side away from the nurse and began to hum a tune.

"Okay," the nurse said as she fixed Gwen's cover, "if you should decide to talk, just ring this bell and I'll come in. I hope you have a good night's sleep." The nurse started to walk to the door when she turned around to Gwen, "Oh, I almost forgot, your boyfriend said he'll be by to pick you up and take you home. Good night."

The nurse closed the door and the room went black.

eighteen

Early the next morning two nurses helped Gwen walk out of her room. Just before exiting the room they looked around to see if anything of Gwen's was left behind. They saw nothing and wondered where her personal belongings were.

"Do you need us to get you anything, Miss Collins? Some water or orange juice?" One of the nurses said.

Gwen was still somewhat groggy from the outpatient procedure they performed last night. She had almost twenty stitches in her head and her left arm was fractured. Gwen was insistent to leave the hospital as soon as possible. The thought of the police stopping by and asking questions frightened her.

Gwen sat in the wheelchair in the front while Jink's friend signed the release papers. Gwen sat still and kept quiet, not wanting to stir things up again. When they got to the car, Gwen recognized one of Jink's friends behind the wheel. As usual, Jink sat upfront on the passenger's side.

Jink turned around occasionally as the car moved slowly from the hospital en route to The Lang Apartments. Gwen and the other woman didn't say anything to each other. Whether Jink was in town or not, it seemed to Gwen as though every woman who knew Jink's name was banned from talking with her. Even as she sat with her head and arm bandaged, things still hadn't changed.

Jink looked back at Gwen just before the car came to a stop directly across the street from her apartment.

"I got some things to do and after I'm done, I'm going home. So, get some rest and I'll talk with you tomorrow. You're lucky, I've decided to give you another chance. I don't do that often. So, take advantage of my kindness."

Jink let Gwen out of the car. He looked at her but didn't say anything when he saw her struggling to stand. Gwen looked at him and knew he looked at her with pity.

The Lang Apartments were just across the street. Jink was going to let her walk by herself, but she looked too pitiful. He walked over to the driver and spoke in a low tone to his friend. He also said something to his acquaintance in the back seat, who rolled down the window in front of him. All Gwen could manage to hear was "I'll be right back. We have to finish our conversation."

Jink walked back over to Gwen and held her arm. They took one slow step at a time. Just as they were about to cross the opposite directional lane, a strange sound came toward them. It came from a 1973 Jaguar.

A man in a chauffeur's hat drove while a black man in a three-piece suit sat in the back seat. This man was flanked by two very beautiful and distinguished looking young women. The car drove by slowly, Both Jink and the man in the back seat stared at each other for a moment. The man put his arms around the two women and he started to grin when he looked at Jink and then Gwen.

*
****

The swanky car belonged to a man by the name of "Mr. Wilson." Mr. Wilson ran the only upscale brothel in Charleston.

For those who were involved in the game of prostitution, or some might say, the "art" of prostitution, there are key players involved whose roles were clearly outlined with borders that are never crossed.

You had "pimps," a generic term and genderless term for a person who was overseeing the business aspects. Although, as in the case of Delores and Big Liz, women were genteelly referred to as "Miss."

Then, you have the "actors" in the play. These were the women, men and transvestites who were paid to make the dreams and desires of the customers come true. These actors went by many names, but what the pimps called them defined their status in the industry. Whether they were "hookers," "prostitutes," or "hoes,' if you were referred to as a "Call Girl," above everything else, you had achieved status.

Finally, there were the customers. A customer was defined by where he or she went. If a customer went to a place like Miss Delores' or Big Liz', he would be called a "Trick." Gwen discovered that more than 90% of these "tricks" were married. They also never gave their names and accepted that the name they heard a prostitute give was also fictitious.

These straight men, primarily, had one thing all in common: they loved the thrill and danger of meeting up secretively with black prostitutes. Some, to the surprise and disgust of Gwen, had many fantasies that they didn't share with their wives and girlfriends or couldn't convince them to go along with it.

The vast majority of these customers were also blue-collar, working-class men. It didn't seem curious to them that they wouldn't give these women the time of day if they should happen to meet in crossing at a department store or a post office, but most certainly, never in the surrounding suburban areas.

The other kind of customer was called, a "John." If you were called a John, it was by the second kind of prostitute called a Call Girl. This was an upscale arrangement. The fees for such arrangements ran anywhere from a few hundred dollars for a couple of hours of time, to several thousand dollars. These "Johns" were buying more than just time, it was understood that they were buying the full experience. And, while hookers in Charleston often set boundaries for what they'd do and wouldn't do, a "Call Girl," and that's what they were at Mr. Wilson's place, were open for anything.

****

Mr. Wilson ran a concealed institution in a large house a few blocks away from the actions on Court Street. On the outside of the establishment written on the marquis, was the name "Edna's Tourist." This private and exclusive arrangement was not open to the general public. There was no outside marketing, nor was there any other types of businesses conducted within the limits of the property.

With the exception of the two women who escorted Mr. Wilson around town from time to time, there was a regular rotation of talented women who came from out of town to facilitate the needs of Wilson's clients.

Wilson's clients were not locals. These were men of social and political distinction that treasured their privacy and paid handsomely for their discretion. There were whispers in the prostitution houses around town that state officials and visiting dignitaries were amongst the visitors to Wilson's place.

Mr. Wilson had strict rules as to who may visit and who may work there. They had to have a sparkling reputation as a professional and as a great performer. This meant that none of the women working in Charleston were able to set foot on Wilson's property, much less, work there.

That was, except Gwen.

****

It had been a couple of hours since Jink had escorted Gwen upstairs to her apartment door. He still didn't want to go in to her "filthy" apartment but making sure she at least made it to her doorstep was satisfactory. He told her that he'd see her later and that he had some business to attend to. Gwen just stood and watched him as he turned around and went downstairs. She locked her apartment door and laid down on the bed. Her head was still throbbing a bit and the bandage wrap kept that blood under submission.

She took off her blouse so she could see her stomach. She saw the black and blue bruises on both of her arms and shoulders, but she couldn't see her stomach while at the hospital. Now, with her blouse off, she saw what was clearly the imprint of his construction boot on her stomach. Gwen touched her side and felt the pain of the boot, but nothing came close to the fear that her unborn child was dead inside of her.

One of the nurses who helped her out of bed this morning also told her that the sonogram came back negative and that there were no signs of permanent injury to her unborn child. Gwen kept this in her mind, but the big bruise mark intimidated her, nonetheless.

Gwen spent a quiet afternoon walking around her room, watching TV, and turning the knob on her radio. Nothing seemed to settle her mind about what happened the night before.

She realized that she needed to get out of the house and visit some friends. 'That's it,' she thought. But as she sat there going through her phonebook and the pages of people who she's called and never received a call back, she thought, 'this might just be a waste of my time'. And so she put down the receiver.

Gwen decided just to take a walk. She wanted to be out but didn't want to see the regulars from Candyman's. As she walked down the street, she decided to get a slice of pizza and a drink. As she walked out of the pizzeria, taking her last bite of food, she remembered two sisters who lived in the area, she just hadn't seen in a long time. 'How would I explain my partially bandaged head? What if they ask if I'm working? What about my pregnancy?'

Gwen hadn't worked out the obvious questions but she did know that these sisters were good, positive people to be around. They laughed a lot and were stunningly beautiful with the olive skin and long, wavy, hair. 'Yes, I'm going to visit Serena and Samantha.'

****

Gwen found the two sisters who lived nearby. When Serena opened the door to the apartment, she let off a scream as loud as a siren. She was so excited to see Gwen standing there. Samantha came running from the other room. In a few minutes, all three women were sitting on the couch and talking as if they were all roommates rehashing the day's events.

Gwen told them about the attempted kidnapping, being assaulted with a crow bar, running for her life, the phone bill situation that got her fired from her job, and her troubles with Jink. The two sisters sat there with their mouths opened.

Serena in particular, was taken with the bruise marks on Gwen's arm. It was at that point that Gwen lifted her shirt and showed them the large footprint bruise on her stomach. Serena got up from the couch and walked to the window. She stared out for a while, saying nothing. Gwen and Samantha looked at each other in bewilderment.

Gwen walked over to Serena, put her arm on her shoulder and gave her a hug, telling her that she's going to be all right.

Serena looked up at Gwen and said,

"I have something to tell you and I don't think you're going like what you hear?"

Gwen remained quiet as a look of alarm came upon her face.

"Gwen," Serena said, "I have a confession to make. Jink's been over here and he comes by here every now and then. I think he likes me."

Samantha stood up,

"But, I don't. I think he's a creep. She can't see that all he wants is her money."

Gwen looked at Serena and was about to respond when the women heard three hard knocks at the door. Samantha turned and as she was unlocking the door, a voice behind it answered,

"Serena and Samantha?"

Samantha opened the door and saw two policemen.

"Yes, how can I help you."

The door was now fully opened. The second policeman spoke,

"We're here to speak to Serena and Samantha."

Serena walked over to the door and stood by Samantha.

"Yes, I'm Serena and this is Samantha, how can we help you?"
"We need for you to come down to the station with us. You're under arrest," the first officer said as he withdrew the handcuffs from his belt.
"Under arrest!" Serena yelled out. "What did we do? We didn't break any laws!"
"Ma'am, we have your names on a list for questioning. Please take some ID's and come with us."

Samantha and Serena looked at each other in horror. Serena looked at the officers,

"Can you at least tell us what you are arresting us for?"
"Ma'am, we need your cooperation," the second officer said.

"When you get to the station, the sergeant on duty will advise you of the situation. You have the right at this moment to remain silent. We have an obligation to report anything you say as evidence in this investigation."

As the policemen were handcuffing Samantha and Serena, Gwen ran to the policemen,

"Officers.... Officers... wait, they didn't commit any crime. I was here with them for the past couple of hours. There must be some mistake," Gwen said as she peered a list attached to a clipboard.
"Who are you?" The first policemen said as he started to walk Samantha out the door.
"My name's Gwen. I've known them for a long time and they're good girls. They don't cause any problems."
"Gwen, huh?" the second policeman said, as he looked at the list. "Gwen Collins?"
"Yes."
"Great! We've been looking for you, too. You're under arrest."

19

Gwen, Samantha and Serena were taken into the police station. They were there with about 50 people that Gwen knew or was familiar with in the club and bar scenes off of Court Street. This included all of the regulars for Candyman's and a club called, The Last Chance.

The sisters' names were soon called and they were taken to another area, leaving Gwen by herself. Gwen managed to hear Jink's real name called in the crowded room, but an officer told the sergeant that he had just been apprehended and was en route to the station.

About an hour and a half later, Gwen's name was called and she was escorted to another area. She was charged as an accomplice to drug trafficking and drug abuse. The sergeant also told Gwen that they were aware that she was an intimate friend of Jink and part of her rehabilitation would require her to end the relationship.

Gwen didn't respond.

Gwen sat in a holding cell for two weeks. She saw almost everyone she knew in Charleston cross by her cell. Terri as well, who was now in the throes of something with one of Delores' workers. Many walked in after Gwen but was processed before her.

A policewoman came to Gwen's holding cell and told her it was time for her to see the judge. Gwen stood in front of the magistrate. The magistrate formally read the charges against her,

"Miss Gwendolyn Collins, it says here that you are charged with violating the Uniform Controlled Substance Act." Then, the judge took off his reading glasses. "Miss... Collins. Ahh, yes, Collins."

Taking a deep breath, the judge looked at Gwen.

"Do you know why you're here?"
"Not really. I didn't do anything."
"You didn't do anything. Uh, huh! Do you know what that fancy term I just read to you means?"
"No, your honor."
"Miss Collins, in simple English, it means that you are being charged with the sale and possession of narcotics."
"No! No... I... I. I'm innocent. I don't sell drugs."
"Miss Collins, people who don't do anything don't get arrested. That's usually how it works. Now, I know there are some cases where innocent people were convicted and served time that they shouldn't. That's unfortunate. But, fortunately for us, we do things a lot differently here. We take Due Consideration very seriously. Do you know what means, Miss Collins?"
"No, your honor. I think I may know but I don't wanna guess."
"Due Consideration is the process by which law enforcement exhausts all of the possibilities of innocence until a judgment is made. If there is a shadow of a doubt, we don't proceed. Now, in

your case, we've been watching the neighborhood and the vicinity around the downtown area for the better part of six months. We know all the people who frequent establishments like Candyman's and The Last Chance to name a few. And, we know that you, in particular, frequent all of the other clubs, bars, juke joints or whatever you want to call them with your part-time boyfriend and pimp, Jink."

"But, your honor, I didn't commit any-"

"Let me finish, Miss Collins. I know that you're from a small town in Kentucky..." The judge put on his reading glasses again and flipped through some papers before looking back up. *"Kentuc- Madisonville! Yes, Madisonville, Kentucky! That's a long way from here, isn't it?"*

"Yes, sir."

"And, what would your mother say if she knew you were hanging out with the people like Jink?"

Gwen stood in silence.

"And, what about your father? What would he think?"

"My father doesn't live with us. I don't talk to him that much."

"Okay, then. This is not about having a pity party. Let's get right down to it. We know.... I know that you use, I should say, abuse drugs. I also know that you're involved with prostitution. And, I also know that you're romantically involved with a married man who's a pimp and whose wife is also involved with his prostitution ring. Do you have anything to say about that?"

Gwen remained silent when the judge looked at her.

"Gwen. I'm your friend. I want you to know that. We kept you in the waiting area until we could process everyone and hopefully gave you time to think about your life and what changes you'd have to make to better yourself if given the opportunity to make a

fresh start for yourself. We don't see you as we see the others. They've been around these parts...most all of their lives and they should know better. We know that you're a stranger and even amongst your so-called friends, you're still treated as an outcast."

"How do you know all of this?" Gwen asked with a bit of skepticism on her face.

The judge looked at Gwen for a moment without saying a word. He looked deep into Gwen's inquiring eyes. He lifted up the stack of papers and pulled out some paper-length photographs. From an angle, Gwen saw the picture of a white man in a t-shirt and baseball cap. He also wore sunglasses in the pictures that were being pulled up. But, Gwen knew him for sure by his smile. One of his two front teeth was chipped off, almost triangular in shape. But, Gwen took to his country smile.

"Do you recognize this man, Miss Collins?"
"Yes, sir. I know him but I can't place where I know him. He does look familiar."
"Miss Collins. This man works for us. And, by us, I mean he works for law enforcement. He works for the F.B.I. He was sent to infiltrate the scene where drug and prostitution activities occur and to let us know who's who and who's doing what. That's how we know, Miss Collins, that you're just a bit player. We're under pressure from the Federal government to get ahead of the drug ring. We... I want to give you an opportunity to turn your life around. I've mulled over your case for a couple of weeks now and I've gone to bed many nights thinking about your situation. I believe somebody above is looking out for you. I strongly suggest, Miss Collins, that you consider your next moves very carefully. You may not always get a good break. Do you understand what I'm trying to say to you, Gwen?"
"I think so sir."

"Okay, I'm going to sentence you to probation provided that you accept these two preconditions. One: you go through our new drug-rehabilitation program. We just built a facility, Guthrie Treatment Center, in Sissonville. The second precondition is this... are you listening very carefully, Miss Collins?"

"Yes, sir. I'm listening carefully."

"The second precondition is that you leave Jink alone. He's trouble and he'll get you into trouble but only you can make these changes, Miss Collins. So, the choice is up to you. Probation is granted if you accept my offer. If you choose not to accept my offer, I am forced to sentence you to jail like the rest of the people we've seen today. So, what is your answer?"

Gwen paused for a moment. She thought it unfair that he would sit there and judge Jink that way. 'He doesn't know him the way I know him. He's not the devil. He can't tell me who to see and who not to see.'

"Your honor, I'm going to accept your offer. I'll go to the treatment center and I'm going to break up with Jink."

"I hope for your sake that you do. And, I'm going to hold you to your promise. Now, hear me clearly, Miss Collins..."

Gwen looked at the judge attentively.

"...if you don't fulfill your time in the treatment center, doing all of the activities that they offer AND if we find that you're keeping company with Jink, you will serve out your entire five-year sentence in prison. Do you understand me?"

"Yes, sir."

The judge stamped some forms in front of him and then looked up to Gwen.

"It is the judgment of this court that we sentence you to a probationary period of five years with a mandatory 12-month period to be served at our drug-rehabilitation center in Sissonville followed by four years of supervised probation with the understanding that you will have no contact whatsoever with Jink. Any violation of these ordinances will result in your incarceration."

The judge signed the forms and handed them to the bailiff. The judge turned away from Gwen and placed Gwen's files on a stack of folders that he lifted from underneath the bench. The policewoman who escorted Gwen tapped Gwen on the shoulder and pointed to the exit. The judge looked at Gwen but said nothing to her as she started to walk away with the guard. Gwen turned back when she reached the door to see the judge but the judge was already walking into his chambers.

****

The Guthrie Treatment Center, the new drug rehabilitation center, was something of a first in the nation. It was one of the first facilities of its kind to treat victims of drug abuse. This was in response to President Nixon's "War on Drugs."

The community's residents protested Sissonville, located in one of the ritzy communities just outside of downtown Charleston. The residents' argued that such a facility would invite crime by putting residents at risk of criminals who'd victimize them to feed their habits, or even worse encourage the lifestyle and behavior of their young people.

There was also a concern that this facility would lower property values. None of those fears ever materialized. If anything, the inmates stayed to themselves in this low-security facility. There were some counselors and security guards but for the most part, inmates kept to themselves. They hung out in the lunch room, played games, socialized or waited for mail from their loved ones.

Guthrie, unfortunately, also became a laboratory for drug experiments. Someone down the corridor from Gwen devised a concoction of spraying Lysol into a can of soda like Coca-Cola to get high.

******

Gwen spent her days and weeks and months going through the same ritual day after day.

When she first arrived in Sissonville, counselors and security guards were very visible around this building on a hill overlooking the city of Charleston. But, as time went by, counselors could be seen napping or playing cards in their office. Security guards, both male and female, were often found socializing with inmates all around campus and even in off-limits areas.

And Gwen missed Jink.

Every day the mail came, she looked forward to a letter or a card from him letting her know that he was thinking of her. It wasn't unreasonable', she thought to herself, because she had done the same for him when he went to Germany. But, no correspondence ever came.

Seeing the drug use and seeing the intimate connections around the building made Gwen think of Jink even more. 'What was he doing? Who was he with? Did he have a new wife-in-law? Was he okay? Was he incarcerated?' All of these questions flooded her mind.

Early one morning, Gwen stayed in bed and thought about the time she had left at the center. She also thought about starting a new life with Jink. She believed that if Jink could see how good he is as a businessman and a manager that he could take those skills and do something legitimate and something profitable. If she could convince Jink that he could make it if he played it straight, then she could show the law enforcement community that Jink was really a good guy after all. Gwen decided that day that it was time to leave the facility.

Leaving the facility was very easy. There was no one patrolling the halls and rooms. The counselors were now not showing up for work and many of the inmates at the facility would be passed out in the dining room area from drugs.

Gwen packed a bag, casually walked out of the facility and down the hill on her way to the city, downtown Charleston.

****

It surprised Gwen that several hours had passed and there were no police sirens going or coming from the facility. As she walked her way back to the city, she "thumbed" a ride back into town.

It was about 8 p.m. when Gwen arrived at Candyman's. The place wasn't as crowded as when she was last there, but she knew this was Jink's home-away-from-home. If he were going to be anywhere, especially having his business meetings, this would be the place.

Gwen looked around the club. She spotted Jink sitting at a table with some other people. His back was toward her, so he didn't see Gwen when she came in. As Gwen walked toward the table, small billows of weed and cigarettes floated above Jink, his friend "Butchie," Jink's new wife-in-law "Mittens" and another woman that Gwen didn't know.

The crowd around Jink stopped talking when Gwen was just a few feet away. From that distance, Gwen heard Jink complaining about how hard it's been to find weed in Charleston. Butchie had just mentioned that there's plenty of weed in Cleveland. Jink sensing something was wrong turned around and saw a smiling Gwen behind him.

"What'cha doing here? You finished your time?" Jink said with a bit of annoyance.
"I thought you'd be glad to see me," Gwen said. "Why didn't you send me a card at least?"
"Send you a card? You know I don't write. Did I ever write back to you when I was in Germany?"

Gwen was about to say something when she recognized that he was telling the truth. She never did receive any replies from him by mail, only phone calls and those were collect.

"I suppose you didn't. Well, aren't you glad to see me?"
"Yeah. Come and sit down. I got business to attend to."

No one said anything to Gwen. But, Butchie looked at Jink and said,

"Jink, Cleveland's got some weed! Woo-hoo! Boy, do they got some weed. My cousin lives in Cleveland and they got imported stuff right from Colombia. Jink, I'm telling you, man. We need to go up to Cleveland and get us some and bring back enough to sell. People are trying to get their hands on some weed and they'll pay anything right now."

"You sure of this, Butchie? You absolutely, 100% sure? 'Cause, I can't be going places and leaving my business left alone too long. You gotta be sure about this."

"*Jink, have I ever lied to you? I'm telling you, man. They got the primo stuff. It'll have you floating above the clouds. You hearin' me?*"

Jink looked at him for a second then he looked around the table, not to look at anyone but to measure out the cost of the trip.

"Okay, let's move on this right away. Okay, let's go."

"Jink... Jink, I can't go," Mittens' said.

"What you mean you can't go. "You goin'," Jink said as he unraveled a few bills from his pocket and threw it on the table. The cigarette hanging from his lips made his refusal sound a bit more intimidating than he wanted it to be.

"Jink, I can't go. I don't want to go. Remember, I still got a family that I go home to at night. I can't be riding around state to state looking for some weed."

Jink looked around to the other woman that Gwen didn't know.

"Are you going or staying," Jink said.

"I'm going with you, Jink. I'll stand by your side." The woman said.

"Well, what about me, Jink?" Gwen said as she gave a hard stare to the woman who was obviously claiming Jink for herself. "That's why I came back... to be with you."

Jink ignored Gwen and waved for the waiter to come. Jink handed the waiter the bills and whispered something in his ear as Butchie had retrieved the car. Jink waved to the bartender and a couple of people he knew as he, Gwen, and his new prostitute got into Butchie's car out front.

The car turned the corner and sped up the street to the expressway and into the dark of night.

20

Jink and Butchie took turns driving up I-77 to Cleveland. The ride was a very long one.

Jink and Butchie talked "shop" the entire time ignoring the women. Gwen and two other women sat silently in the backset. The two women would occasionally whisper amongst themselves, but not to Gwen.

During the ride, Gwen noticed one of the women slowly sliding her hands in her bag and taking out a small plastic bag with a white powder in it. Once the woman had the bag concealed in her fist, she turned to see if Gwen was watching her. Gwen would always turn her face to the window as if to pretend to be taken with the landscape.

The woman closest to Gwen poured the powder into rows onto the back of her hand. Each woman bent their head down, out of Jink's and Butchie's sight, and took a hit. The men were still busy talking unaware of what was happening directly behind them.

Gwen didn't know how Jink couldn't tell what was going on. After each woman took their hit and covered their nostrils with their opened hand, the women began talking a bit louder. Did the coke affect their hearing? In any case, Gwen was the only one not part of any conversation

The woman closest to her began laughing incessantly about stories of other drug users and their lack of effectively snorting coke. She and the other woman found this to be a hysterical conversation. But the woman next to Gwen, kept making annoying whistling sound every time she inhaled. It was like a dog whistle coming out of an alley cat's mouth. This annoying sound went on for almost a half an hour before Gwen leaned over to see where that noise was coming from. As Gwen leaned forward in her seat and looked around at the ladies, she was able to catch a glimpse of the women's faces. As they had their heads back from laughing, Gwen was able to see their noses. Both of them had about a dime-sized hole in their nostrils.

Gwen slowly pulled herself back to her place and looked out the window, but this time, it was for real. She needed to think about this drug connection and its hold on everyone around her.

****

It was just after they crossed the border into Ohio that Jink insisted on stopping to get a hit. No one objected, but Butchie told Jink that they still had a long way to go and this will delay them through the morning. Jink said nothing as he went into his bag and pulled out a bunch of small plastic bags, a long thin rubber tube and a needle.

"You think we really got time for this now?" Butchie said to Jink as Jink tapped the door of the car calling for the women to come out.

"Look at this, Butchie, my man! Just look at this!" Jink said as he looked up at the night sky off to the side of any empty interstate.

He looked up to the sky and walked in circles.

"You see this, Butchie? Huh, this is us! This is me... I'm free. I'm free as the stars that sit in the sky. Can't nobody take away my freedom!" Jink looked around to everyone, "Hey, let's not waste this moment. Let's get a hit! We've all been dry since before we left Charleston. I know y'all must be hungry now!"

Gwen looked at the girls who giggled to themselves. They walked up to Jink, each putting their arm around the other's shoulder. Butchie was lighting up a joint while he handed Jink a big bag from the front seat.

This was Jink's magic bag. He had a little of everything, but Gwen knew if given the choice Jink would choose heroin because it made him mellow and a bit more understanding. Gwen spoke softly in Jink's ear that she'd prefer to do heroin and save the other stuff for later. Jink looked around and agreed. Gwen thought he figured out if they were pulled over tonight, Jink would be too antsy to stay calm.

"You right, Gwen. I don't need to tempt fate. Let's do one hit of the horse and get back on the road." Jink said as he looked into Gwen's eyes.

As Gwen and Jink sat by themselves on the grass taking hits of heroin, the two women and Butchie laid on the grass staring at the sky. Gwen guessed that they did a "Speedball" since that was Butchie's mixture of choice.

While everyone was enjoying the high, Gwen crept up from her spot next to Jink who didn't notice that she wasn't laying beside him. Gwen walked over to the car and was amazed that very few cars passed by, none of them being a police car. Gwen quickly realized that there were four people right in front of her laying on the grass and enjoying a high. But, what if a policeman came by? How would they explain their situation? And, what if there's now a warrant for her leaving the drug treatment center a few hours ago? She recognized that she'd face additional charges because now they'd also have her for drug possession and being in the company of Jink.

Gwen went into her bag and withdrew the leftovers from her milk. She leaned over and found a couple of needles in the ashtray and sat back in the seat. She tried blowing it, then brushing off the tip of the needle by grazing it on her pants. She was about to inject herself when she saw a rubber band on the floor next to her feet. She reached down and picked it up. She pulled the band over her arm near the inside of her elbow so that she could get a clear shot of her vein. Fifteen minutes after she injected herself, Gwen was ready to head to Cleveland and so was everyone else.

****

On the ride there, Jink explains about the culture within the drug world.

This mindset is really a sophisticated level of "street knowledge." One has to have this in order to survive and to protect themselves from the elements, such as knowing what were the "good" drugs and "bad" drugs.

When Jink introduced Gwen to the different kinds of drugs that he used, he also warned her about the stories and pitfalls in becoming an addict or a junkie.

Jink made most of his money through prostitution, which he finally admitted to Gwen. He showed her some of the girls that worked for him, including his legal wife and another woman who didn't come around as much, and one whom Jink also called his wife-in-law.

And like the prostitution game, there were do's and don'ts. Where to hustle and where not to hustle. What to look out for and where the safe places were to transact. The hardest part of it all is knowing how to distinguish someone who's from law enforcement and someone who's a new customer.

The weekenders, as he pointed out worked during the week and came to Court Street or Summers Street for a weekend high only. Typically they spent their disposable income, which on average was about $100.

An "addict" was someone who used drugs very frequently and needed it to get over some kind of emotional hump.
And, a "junkie" was someone who lost all sense of reality and only wanted the images of a different kind of life.

Gwen admitted to Jink that she loved getting high off of marijuana because it made her feel as if she were a much better singer than she was. In reality, she realized that her singing hadn't gotten better, but she was still in the same place where she was before the first hit.

The drug scene in Charleston was not as neat as categorizing behaviors based on use. It was, in Gwen's mind, a very complicated subject. As she would listen to conversations she would learn about the different types of drugs.

She heard about certain kinds like "Black Beauty" and "Black Molly" and how these drugs would "pop" your heart. She'd also hear about junkies dying after taking one hit too many and collapsing dead. Their bodies would be dragged from those private drug spots and thrown in an alley or in a trash bin for someone to find them. The fear was that if someone was with them, they could and usually were charged with an accessory.

In New York, the police could charge someone with "Internal" possession of narcotics and West Virginia was also considering enacting the same laws.

There were two main drugs that everyone wanted. All of the drug dealers had access to it in addition to marijuana and that was heroin and cocaine.

Everybody who was anybody in the clubs in Charleston experimented with every kind of drug at least once. Psychedelic or "acid" drugs like LSD, were as Jink called them, "white folks drugs." It was only when Jimi Hendrix popularized it that blacks in Charleston became curious about its effects.

For her part, Gwen preferred heroin because of the 30-minute euphoria she experienced when she used it. Cocaine gave her a rush but she became alarmed when she'd see Jink having extreme muscle tension in his jaw. He'd begin to chew on his tongue and sometimes would have uncontrollable salivation.

She used to dissuade Jink from following up the high with another fix or several planned fixes by telling him that they could do it later because they had places to go and people to see. It was a temporary solution, but he'd make up for lost opportunities later.

****

Butchie finally pulled up in front of his cousin's house later on in the morning. Everyone in the car was sleeping, but it took Jink only a moment to wake up and start snapping his fingers at the women in the back seat.

Everyone was laid out on the couch in the living room, while Butchie and his cousin talked in the kitchen. Jink wanted to know where he could go to find some action. The cousin told Jink and Butchie that they could find whatever they wanted on Euclid Avenue!

"Euclid Avenue?" Jink said.
"Yeah, anything you want and anything you could think of is on Euclid," the cousin said, "but you had better wait until it gets dark 'cause that when all of the good stuff starts showing up."

Jink smiled,

"That's good to know."

Jink tapped Butchie on the shoulder and told him he'd be in the living room when he was finished talking to his cousin. But that really meant for Butchie to cut the conversation short and meet him in the living room immediately. Jink looked at the women and thought about how much money he could make if he played his cards right. Jink looked at Gwen,

"You think you can handle these two women for me?"
"Me?" Gwen said. "I can't handle them. They only follow what you say."

Jink looked at the other women who were sitting on a couch

horizontal from where he was kneeling,

"I ain't gonna say this but once. I want you three to go out there and find out how much weed is out there, how much "horse" and how much "Coke" is out there." Pointing to Gwen, "I'm leaving this woman in charge, you do whatever it is she tells you to do. You got that?"

"Jink, honey. Where are we going and what's up with this woman telling us what to do?" One of the women said.
"Your job ain't to ask questions. Your job is to do what I tell you to do. That's it. You don't have to think because I just did it for you." Jink said angrily as his eyebrows furled by his anger.

None of the women who sat together responded. They looked at Gwen with a blank face then turned their heads and looked out the window.

It was about nine-thirty in the evening when Jink and Butchie walked back into the living room from a few hours before.

"Okay, get up. Me and Butchie got some things to do. Y'all gonna have to walk down the hill and make it over to Euclid. Gwen..."

Gwen looked up at Jink,

"Hey!"
"Gwen, take some of these dimes and call me and let me know where you're at and we'll come get you," Jink said as he fished in his pocket. He took out a bundle of coins and rested the entire pile in Gwen's open hands. Jink leaned close to Gwen and spoke very softly in her ears away from the other women.
"If you see there's some action jumping off, send one of the

girls to make it happen. I want double the price of what we charge back home. Send them out, but I don't want you running off with anyone. You be my eyes, got it?"

Gwen smiled,

"I got it."

****

Gwen was more nervous than carefree. She realized that she was in a much bigger and tougher city than Charleston. She had the same trepidations when she came to Charleston from Madisonville. This same fear had now revisited her.

The women made it down the long winding hill when they saw several women walking around. Gwen thought it looked like a television version of 'how a prostitute should look with long boots, very short skirts and too much makeup.' Gwen looked at herself and the other two women who were with her and felt they were overdressed for that neighborhood.

They stood there for a while just talking small talk amongst themselves when Gwen noticed one of the prostitutes talking with a man standing on the other side of the street. The women pointed in Gwen's direction and then looked back at the man.

The man, dressed in a full-length mink and calf-high Napa leather zip-up boots came walking over very briskly, looking around Gwen and the other women before turning back to Gwen,

"What you doing out here? Where's your man?"
"What do you mean, where's my man? I ain't got no man, why do you ask?" the woman with a whistling nostril answered.

"Oh, I see. You got a mouth on you. Well, I'll tell you what. I'm gonna give you five minutes to produce your man or I'm gonna be your man and you gonna give me some papers tonight," the pimp said as his women behind him started to laugh.

Gwen took a step toward him,

"Sir, we're from out of town. We don't mean no harm. We're just trying to find out where we could go to get something to drink."
"That's it...something to drink. You out here all this time 'cause you thirsty?" He said and he turned around and laughed with his women. "Well, I'll tell you this. Why don't you keep walking, and that way, I don't make the mistake of thinking you're trying to take over my turf."

Gwen grabbed the other two women who continued to stare at the pimp and blow bubbles in his direction.

"Keep up with me!" Gwen said as she quickly walked away.

In her direction, Gwen saw a gas station coming into view a couple of blocks away. As the women made it to the gas station grounds, Gwen looked around for a phone booth to call Jink, fearing what would happen if they had to walk past the pimp again on their way back up the hill.

From a distance, a tall, somewhat stocky man who looked like he was in his 50's finished pumping his gas and walked casually over to Gwen. He had brown eyes, but the wrinkles under his eyes showed both sadness and fatigue as if the extra weight he carried was a reflection of worries he carried in his soul.

"I'm sorry to bother you. But, could I ask you a question?"

"Me?" Gwen said as she looked around to the other women with her.

"Yes, you!" he said.

He walked a few feet away signaling the question was only for Gwen to hear personally. Gwen quickly looked at the other women, then walked up to the man.

"I'm sorry, sir, but I'm not from around here, I don't know where anything is."

"Can I be your slave?" he said with a stone impression.

"WHAT! Say what? Did I... excuse me, what did you just say?"

"I said, can I be your slave?"

"My slave?"

"Yes. I want to be your slave."

"Oh, my god. This can't be happening," Gwen said as she turned around to see the look of shock on the other women's faces.

Before she could turn back to answer the man who bore a striking resemblance to Rob Reiner, Jink and Butchie pulled into the gas station. It seemed like they drove in slow motion. The expression on Jink's face when he saw the man standing in front of Gwen was one of unmistakable concern.

"Excuse me," the man interrupted Gwen from looking at Jink, "what's your name?"

"My name...oh... my name is Lynn...Lynn Johnson."

"Well, Miss Johnson, can I be your slave?"

Before Gwen could respond, she heard Jink call her.

"Excuse me, sir. I'll be right back." Gwen quickly ran to Jink who stood staring at the man.

He was at least a foot and half taller than Jink, and easily one hundred and twenty pounds heavier.

"What's this I hear about this fool?" Jink said.
"I don't know. We just came here to get away from that pimp who was threatening us up the block and we decided to get something to drink. That's when this gentleman asked me if he could be my slave."
"He asked you what?" Jink said as he stared in the man's direction.
"He asked me if he could be my slave," Gwen said as she shrugged her shoulders.
"What does that fool want?"
"How do I know? We just got here about two minutes before you." Gwen responded.

Jink and Butchie walked past Gwen and the other women. Jink walked up to the man and stared him in the face. Butchie stood next to Jink also staring him in the face but not attempting to say anything.

Jink lifted his head and nodded to the man,

"What's your beef?"

The man said nothing.

"You got some beef with us. My women did anything to you they ain't telling me?"

The man stood silent.

"You want to be my slave? Okay, give me your wallet."
The man didn't inch, staring through Jink's eyes.

Gwen grabbed Jink by the arm.

"Jink, I didn't say he was trying to harm me. He seems very gentle. I think he's lonely and wants to be friends."

Jink looked at Gwen,

"We ain't got time for friends. We're here on business. Come over here for a second Gwen, let me shout something at you."

Jink walks a few feet away when Gwen comes over.

"You think this fool got any money?"
"How would I know? I don't know the man. I just met him."
"Go get his wallet," Jink said.
"Get his wallet? How am I gonna get his wallet?"
"Tell him to give you his wallet."
"Say what!"
"Go over there and tell that fool to give you his wallet."

Gwen walked over to the man a couple of times looking back to Jink as if to verify this is what she's supposed to be doing.

"Excuse me, sir, can I have your wallet?"

Jink, a few feet back screamed,

"Don't ask him for his wallet. Tell him to give you his wallet!"
"Excuse me, sir, could you please give me your wallet?"

After Gwen had said that, she heard a sigh behind her and heard Jink's voice again.

"He's your slave. You don't ask permission of a slave. You tell them what to do. Don't you know your history?"

Frustrated because she didn't want to hurt or humiliate the man and fearing that she may disappoint Jink again, Gwen took a deep breath and put out her hand,

"GIVE ME YOUR WALLET."

The man looked at Gwen for a second, then answered

"*Yes, my master,*" as he reached into his back pocket and gave Gwen his wallet.

Gwen's hand shook as she slowly turned around and walked back to Jink. Butchie, who was watching from afar, ran over to Jink as did the other women, who began chatting amongst themselves at what was unfolding. Gwen started to peek into his wallet when she noticed Jink about to raise his hand to take the wallet from her.

"No! This is mine!" Gwen said.

She fully opened the wallet and removed the bills. A quick glance and Gwen was about two hundred dollars richer. Jink stared at the man who didn't move a muscle as Gwen was stuffing the cash in her back pocket. Jink walked over to the man and asked,

"You got any more money?"

The man stood silent. Jink ran back to Gwen,

"Ask that fool is he has any more money?"

Gwen walked over to the man and took a deep breath,

"Do you have any more money?"
"Yes, my master."
"Gwen," Jink called.

Gwen walked back to Jink.

"He says he has more money but I don't think he can get it now because the bank is closed until tomorrow morning."

Jink looked around and saw the gentleman's late model Oldsmobile still parked by the gas pump.

"Gwen, tell that fool to give you his car."
"Say, what? You want me to ask him for his car? I can't do that. How's he supposed to get home?"
"Listen to me. We've got to get back to Charleston, tell that fool to give you his car."

Gwen walked slowly to the man.

"Give me your car. I need it to get home to Charleston tomorrow."

As the man reached into his pocket for the keys, he looked up to Gwen and said,

"I want to go with you."
"You want to go with me?"
"Yes, my master."
"Oh, my god! This is crazy!" Gwen walked back over to the group. "He wants to drive us back to Charleston tomorrow. We got to take him to stay with us at Butchie's cousin's place tonight."

There was a lot of chatter about what was going on but Jink told

Gwen in the midst of melee that if they played their cards right, they could get a lot of money out of him as well as his car.

"Yeah, tell him he's coming with you tonight," Jink said, with a smile on his face.

Both cars were parked out in front of Butchie's cousin's house while everyone from the Charleston group was in the living room. All night, they tormented and mocked the man, while Gwen tried to diffuse the comments by changing the subject, although she privately thought to herself, there was no way to fully protect him. 'What if he had a knife or a gun? What happens if he came back and stole everything in this house?'

"Okay, Gwen, it's time to go to bed," Jink said, as he felt his eyes closing in on him. "But I got one more question for that fool. I want to see him mop this floor with an ice cube with his nose."

"Yeah," Butchie said, as the other women in the room laughed.

Jink looked at the guy,

"Go in the kitchen, get an ice cube from the refrigerator and mop the floor with your nose."

The man didn't move. Jink told him again and received no response before Jink realized his mistake.

"Gwen, tell that fool to mop the floor."

Gwen got up from the chair and went over to the man.

"Listen, I want you to mop the floor with your nose. Go to the kitchen, get an ice cube out of the fridge and bring it back here."

The man did as Gwen told him to. He brought back the ice but kept the ice cube in his palm.

"Okay, I want you to get on all fours and push that ice cube with your nose across the length of this room. Afterward, I want you to sit down by yourself in that corner."

The man did just as Gwen asked of him. Then he sat on a chair a corner of the room. Gwen looked at Jink,

"Are you satisfied?"

The group made an early start, and Jink insisted on the guy buying gas for both cars during the trip. During the ride, Gwen asked, then told the man to stop at the bank and withdraw five hundred dollars. When Jink saw the man return from the bank, he insisted that the man give him the money, but the man looked at Jink with a blank expression. Gwen took the bundle of money and put it in her bosom.

The trip back to Charleston seemed to be a lot shorter than the trip up to Cleveland, but Gwen enjoyed riding in the man's cream colored Olds. The leather seats and bigger windows made quite an impression on her.

The group made it back to Charleston in the early evening hours. Jink, who was driving the man's car with Gwen and the man in the back, looked out of his window and told Butchie he needed to stop at a particular bar up the street. Gwen didn't clearly hear what he was saying to Butchie as her mind was on how the man was going to get back home if Jink forces her to tell the man to turn over the keys permanently.

Jink and Butchie parked the cars, got out and spoke for a few minutes before Jink looked at the two women,

"Okay, back to work, vacation's over. Make sure you make my numbers since you ain't been to work for a few days. I ain't running no charitable service here."

"Jink, Jink!" Gwen called from the car, "What are we going to do about him?"

"Tell him to go home. I got work to do," Jink said as he started walking up the street, leaving Gwen and the man.

Gwen gave him his keys,

"Wait right here until I come back. I'll only be gone a few minutes."

"Yes, my master," he said as Gwen paused for a second not believing it was real.

Gwen ran up the street trying to catch up with Jink, glancing in the different clubs that he might have stopped in. She was approaching Candyman's when she heard some footsteps walking quickly in her direction. She turned around and saw two black policemen gaining on her.

"COLLINS! COLLINS!"

At the last minute, Gwen decided not to disappear in the crowded, darkness of Candyman's, that night. She turned and ran across the street, hoping to get to the open field when Dallas Staples and Harvey Bush grabbed her and handcuffed her against a car.

"Collins, you can make this easy on yourself or you can make it rough on yourself," Officer Staples said.

"All we want Collins is to know where he is," Officer Bush said.

"Who?" Gwen said.

"You know who," Bush said.

"NO! I don't know you're talking about. You didn't even tell me why you're arresting me."

"Collins we don't want you. We're looking for Jink and we know that you know his whereabouts."

"I'm telling you. I haven't seen him. I'm looking for him now. Please let me go. I'm pregnant and you're pressing me against the car."

Officer Staples pulled her from away from the car and walked her to their squad car.

'All you have to do is stay calm, Gwen. They're looking for Jink, not you.' These were the thoughts Gwen began thinking to herself. She kept the thought that they'd come back and let her off with a warning. Officers Staples and Bush walked back to the door, both leaning in on different sides.

"Miss Collins. Can you tell us where Jink is?" Staples said.

"I told you," Gwen said, "I don't know where he is."

"That's fine. We regret to inform you that we found your name on a database of parole violations, more specifically there's been an arrest warrant out for your arrest for running away from the treatment center," Bush said, as he reached into his side pouch and took out a pen and pad.

"Miss Collins," Staples said, "*You're under arrest for parole violation.*"

"I'm not brave, but after reading A Journey Begins, I said to myself, I too have a journey. A lot different from you, but a pretty wild one. I have to read book TWO cause I'm looking forward to reading more about Jink. I have to find out about the jerks you ran from."

– Marty.Holley@

"Chapter 6 was enlightening. Chapter 6 was very emotional for me. was saddened to learn that a person in the neighborhood that everyone knew and trusted was molesting the children."

– An Amazon reader

"I read the good journey of One and it literally touched every emotio that I have. I went from tears to laughter. I felt pain and joy. I also fe the emotions that Gwen felt which made the book become alive for me. It also made me want to read the next book. I felt that if Gwen could start this journey, just maybe there is hope for others."

– Michael L.

"I was delighted when Gwen Womack published the inspiring and edifying account of her personal experiences with God's indescribabl grace! I am equally excited to anticipate the blessings of her next volume, in which she describes the marvelous manner in which He ha continued to unfold His mission and ministry for her life!"

– Dr. Larry Gilliam, Ed. D., Ph.D., Ex. Dir., Daysprings Counseling Daysprings Institute.

www.ingramcontent.com/pod-product-compliance
Lightning Source LLC
Chambersburg PA
CBHW020651300426
44112CB00007B/337